② Ombre's rainbow tones have a
spring freshness in these pastel
shades.
★ Knit with "Sport Yarn"
★ Directions on page 65.
AF327806
2

③ A simple pattern becomes sensational in this multi-colored yarn.
★ Knit with "Bulky Yarn"
★ Directions on page 66.

④ An understated classic—this gray pullover completes our monocromatic fashion scheme.
★ Knit with "Sport Yarn"
★ Directions on page 67.

⑤ This high-quality tweed will enliven your prettiest sportswear.
★ Knit with "Sport Yarn"
★ Directions on page 68.

⑥ There's no nonsense about the sophistication of this drop-shouldered gray pullover.
★ Knit with "Bulky Yarn"
★ Directions on page 69.

6

8

⑦ Here's a feminine tweed cardigan
you'll want to live in.
★ Knit with "Bulky Yarn"
★ Directions on page 70.
⑧ A distinctive tweed makes this a
stylish substitute for a jacket.
★ Knit with "Bulky Yarn"
★ Directions on page 71.

9

10

⑨ The basic good looks of this vest will do wonders for your favorite tailored sports ensembles.
★ Knit with "Bulky Yarn"
★ Directions on page 12.
The matching men's pullover capi-talized on this design.
Knit with "Bulky Yarn"
Directions on page 13.

10

Paired Lifestyles

MATERIALS: "Bulky Yarn" 390g ash gray. 4 buttons 1.7cm in diameter.
NEEDLES: Knitting needles No. 8 and No. 6.
SIZES: Bust ... 94.5cm. Width across back measurement ... 41cm. Length ... 53cm.
GAUGE: 18 sts and 24 rows in 10cm square over pattern A to C.
DIRECTIONS: Make foundations ch sts with another yarn, using crochet hook and transfer sts. from the wrong side of ch to No. 8 needles. Repeat pattern A to C, changing every 22 rows as shown in the chart. In case of decreasing over 2 sts to shape armholes, bind off sts at the beginning of rows; work the right end on the front side and the left end on the back side. Also work at the beginning of rows alternately to cast off sts of shoulder slope, referring to page 74. After shaping body, make rib for lower border. Change to No. 6 needles and knit 2 sts at each end. Join shoulder seam inside out with sl st using crochet hook. Pick up sts from body to make neck and center band as shown below. Make buttonholes on the right side band of work facing.

★ **Shown on page 10.**

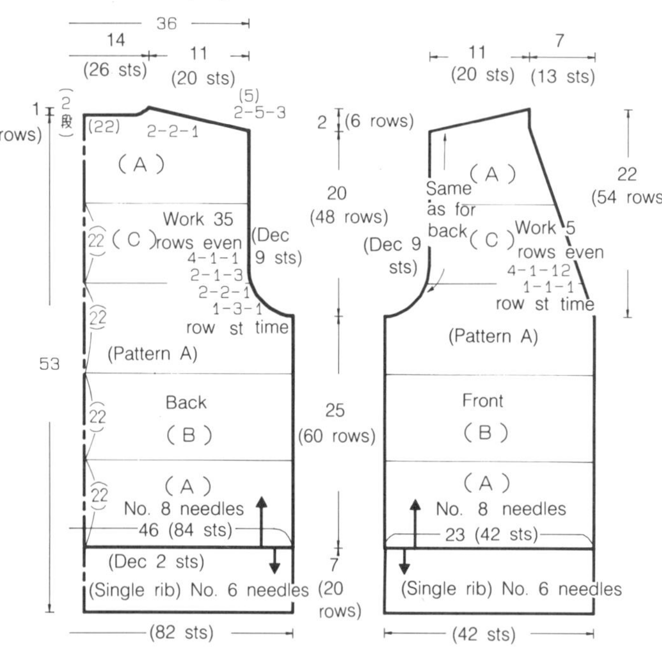

Neck, center, and arm band

(Single rib) No. 6 needles

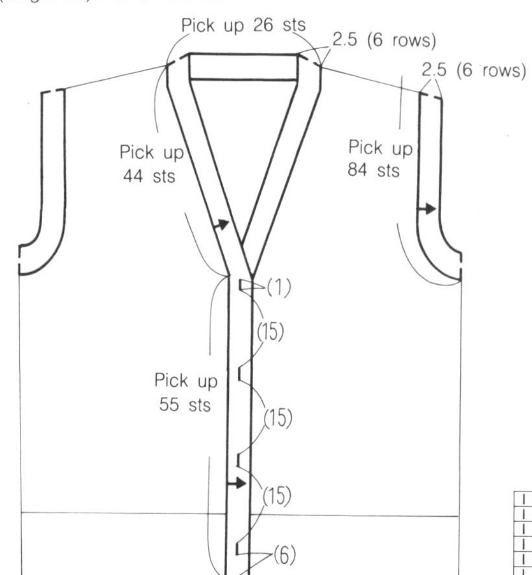

Pattern chart A to C

C

B

A

☐ = purl st

Start of back and front body

Buttonhole

MATERIALS: "Bulky Yarn" 780g ash gray.
NEEDLES: Knitting needles No. 8 and No. 6
SIZES: Chest ... 104cm. Length ... 63.5cm. Center of neck to wrist measurement ... 78cm.
GAUGE: 18 sts and 24 rows in 10cm square over patterns A and B.
DIRECTIONS: Place pattern A at the center of body and sleeves and work symmetrically as shown. Make ch sts with another yarn using crochet hook, and transfer sts from wrong loop of ch to No. 8 needle. Transferred sts are counted in the first row, start pattern from row 2. Work rows even up to neckline, marking the point of underarms. Place remaining center 1 st on holder, and work right and left front separately, decreasing sts to shape neckline. Increase sts to shape sleeves, lifting the loop lying 1 st inside both ends of previous rows. Unfasten the foundation ch of body and sleeves, picking up sts to work rib toward opposite ends. Join shoulder seam inside out with sl st using crochet hook. Set sleeves in body, grafting sts and rows, referring to the diagram on page 73. Work neck band knitting 1 st in center.

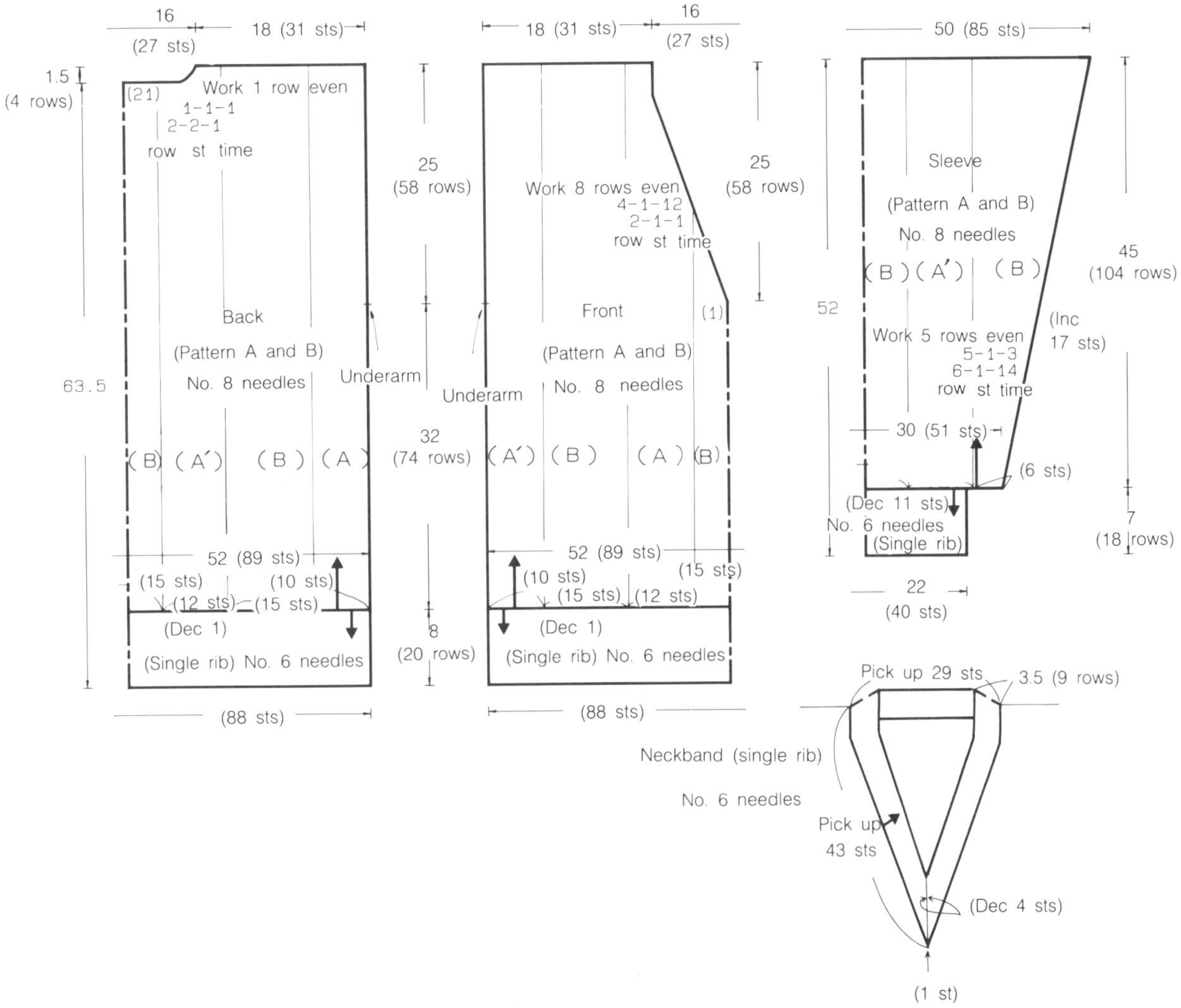

★ **Shown on page 11.**

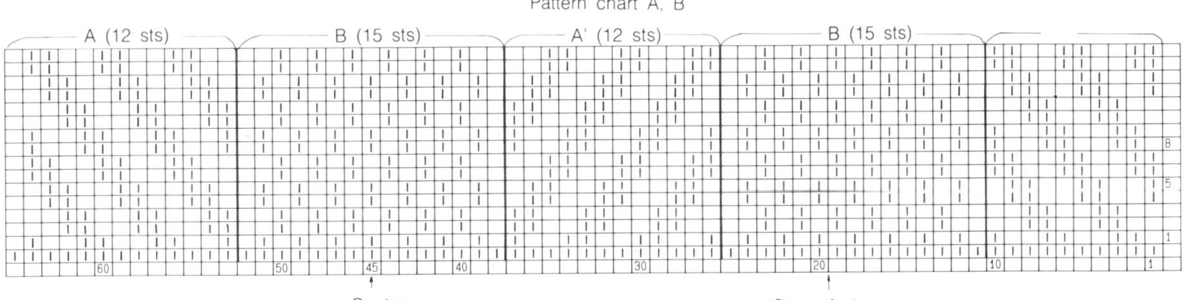

11

⑪ Comfortable good looks is the feature of this Italian-style striped pullover.
★ **Knit with "Bulky Yarn"**
★ **Directions on page 16.**
⑫ The superb matching vest adds carmine red for a chic contrast.
★ **Knit with "Bulky Yarn"**
★ **Directions on page 17.**

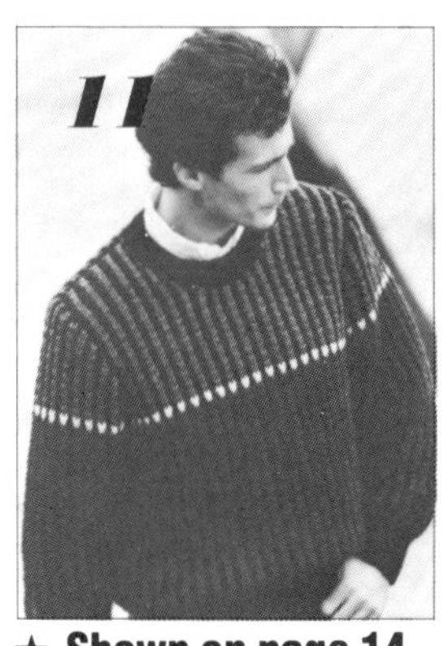

MATERIALS: "Bulky Yarn" 360g black, 190g bluish purple, 90g green, and 10g white.

NEEDLES: Knitting needles No. 8 and No. 6.

SIZES: Chest ... 104cm. Width across back ... 42cm. Length ... 69cm. Outside sleeve ... 60cm.

GAUGE: 11 sts and 32 rows in 10cm square over patterns A to C.

DIRECTIONS: Work the same in patterns A to C, but change colors from bluish purple to white and to green. Make ch sts with another yarn using crochet hook and transfer sts from wrong side of ch to No. 8 needle. Work pattern referring to diagram shown on opposite page. Work 122 rows up to underarm, then decrease sts for armholes. In decreasing over 2 sts, bind off sts alternately at the beginning of rows. After shaping shoulder, place remaining sts on separate holders for shoulder seam and neckline. Work front the same as back. Increase sts to shape shoulder, lifting loop lying 1 st inside both ends of the previous row. Unfasten the foundation ch and work rib for body and wrist band. Join shoulder seam with sl st using crochet hook, and work neckband. Set sleeves neatly in body inside out with sl st.

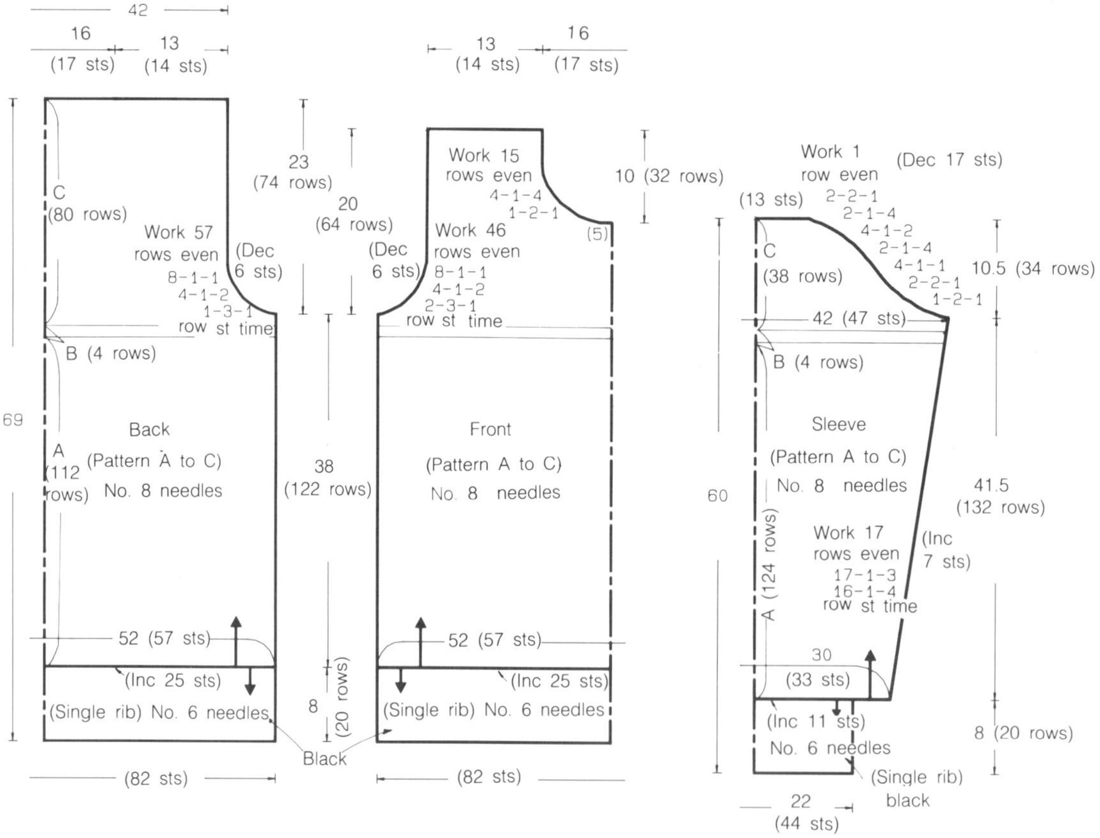

★ **Shown on page 14.**

Pattern chart

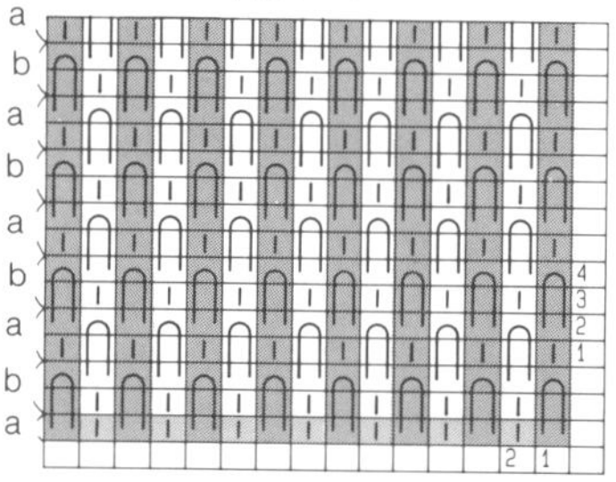

Color chart

	a	b
C	Black	Green
B	Black	White
A	Black	Bluish purple

Neckband (Single rib) No. 6 needles

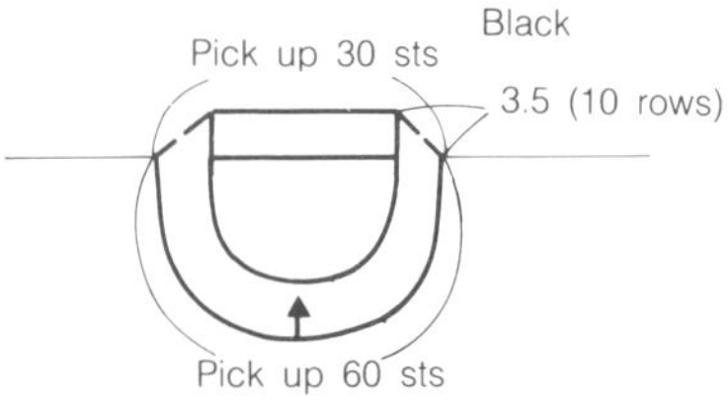

★ **Shown on page 15.**

MATERIALS: "Bulky Yarn" 180g black, 65g bluish purple, 45g each of red, green, and 10g white.

NEEDLES: Knitting needles No. 8 and No. 6.

SIZES: Bust ... 94cm. Width across back measurement ... 40cm. Length ... 60cm.

GAUGE: 11 sts and 32 rows in 10 cm square over pattern A to C.

DIRECTIONS: Work same in pattern A to D, but change colors from bluish purple to white to red and to green. Make ch sts with another yarn using crochet hook, and transfer sts from wrong side of ch to No. 8 needle. Work sts referring to diagram shown below, making vertical stripe of every other st. In decreasing over 2 sts, bind off sts at the beginning of rows alternately. After shaping shoulder, place remaining sts on separate holders for shoulder seam and back neckline. Unfasten the foundations ch of body, and pick up sts to work single rib toward opposite end. Join shoulder seam inside out with sl st using crochet hook. Pick up sts for neck and arm band as shown in diagram, then work rib circularly.

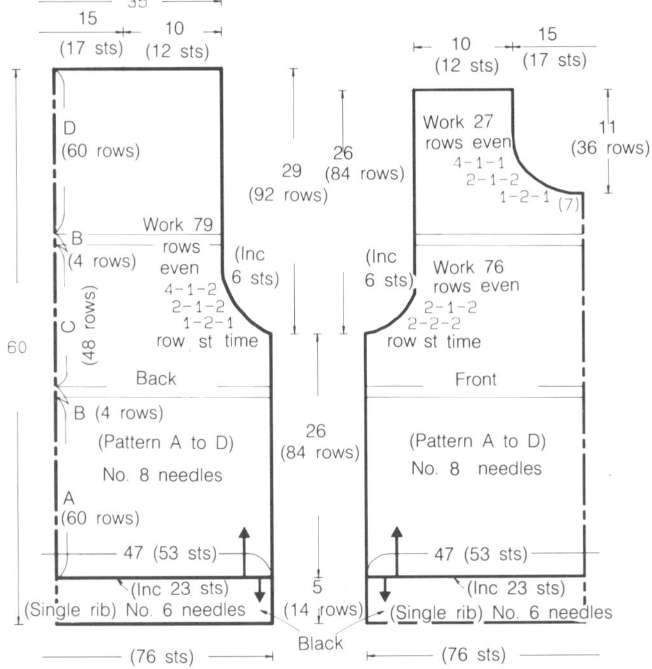

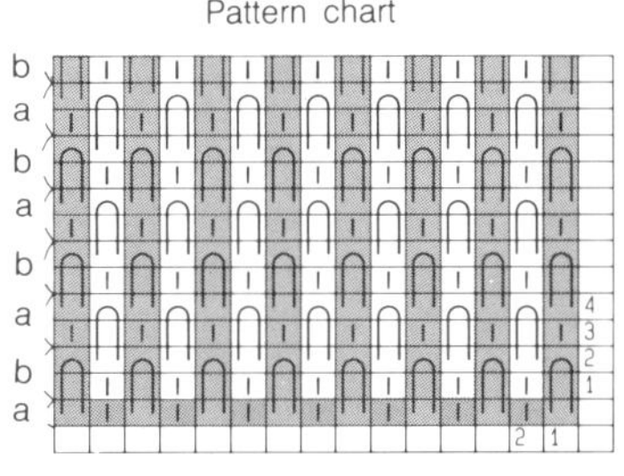

Color chart

	a	b
D	Black	Green
C	Black	Red
B	Black	White
A	Black	Bluish purple

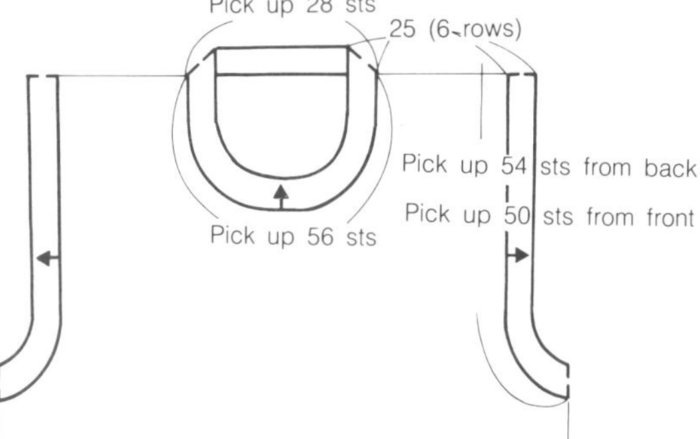

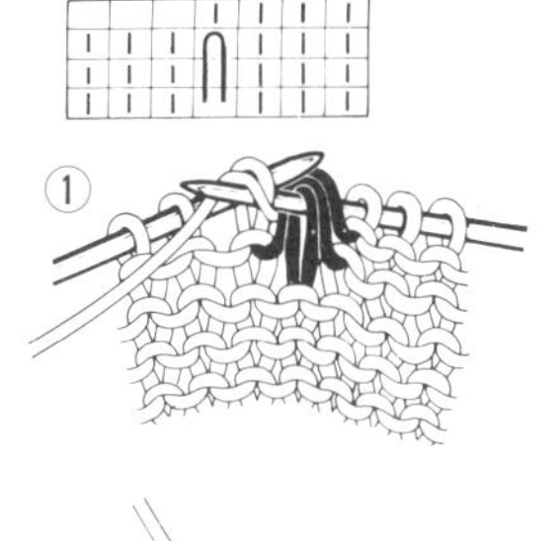

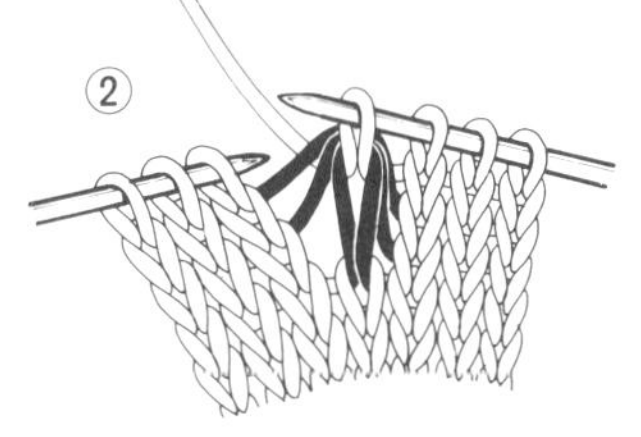

⑬ Make this man's pullover in one of
the basic colors chosen from her
sweater.
★ Knit with "Bulky Yarn"
★ Directions on page 20.
⑭ Wonderful colors and texture
enliven this patchwork sweater.
★ Knit with "Bulky Yarn"
★ Directions on page 21.
14
19

★ **Shown on page 18.**

MATERIALS: "Bulky Yarn" 780g yarn variegated color of gray. Turkish blue, gold, violet, pink, etc.

NEEDLES: Knitting needles No. 10½ and No. 8.

SIZES: Chest ... 108cm. Width across back measurement ... 42cm. Length ... 63.5cm. Outside sleeve ... 59cm.

GAUGE: 10.5 sts and 15 rows in 10 cm square over stockingette st.

DIRECTIONS: Make ch sts with another yarn using crochet hook for lower border and wrist, and transfer sts from wrong side of ch, using No. 10½ needle.

Back: Work sts even until row 52. Bind off sts at the beginning of row alternately to decrease over 2 sts for armholes. Work remaining sts to shape shoulder slope as shown on page 74.

Front: Work same as for back. Place 9 remaining center sts of front on holder to shape neckline, and work right and left separately decreasing sts.

Sleeve: Increase sts to shape sleeve, lifting loop lying 1 st inside both ends of previous row. Bind off sts at beginning of row to shape cap alternately.

Finishing: Join shoulder seam inside out, working sl st with crochet hook; then work neckband. Sew side and sleeve seams with overcasting stitch, and set sleeves using sl st.

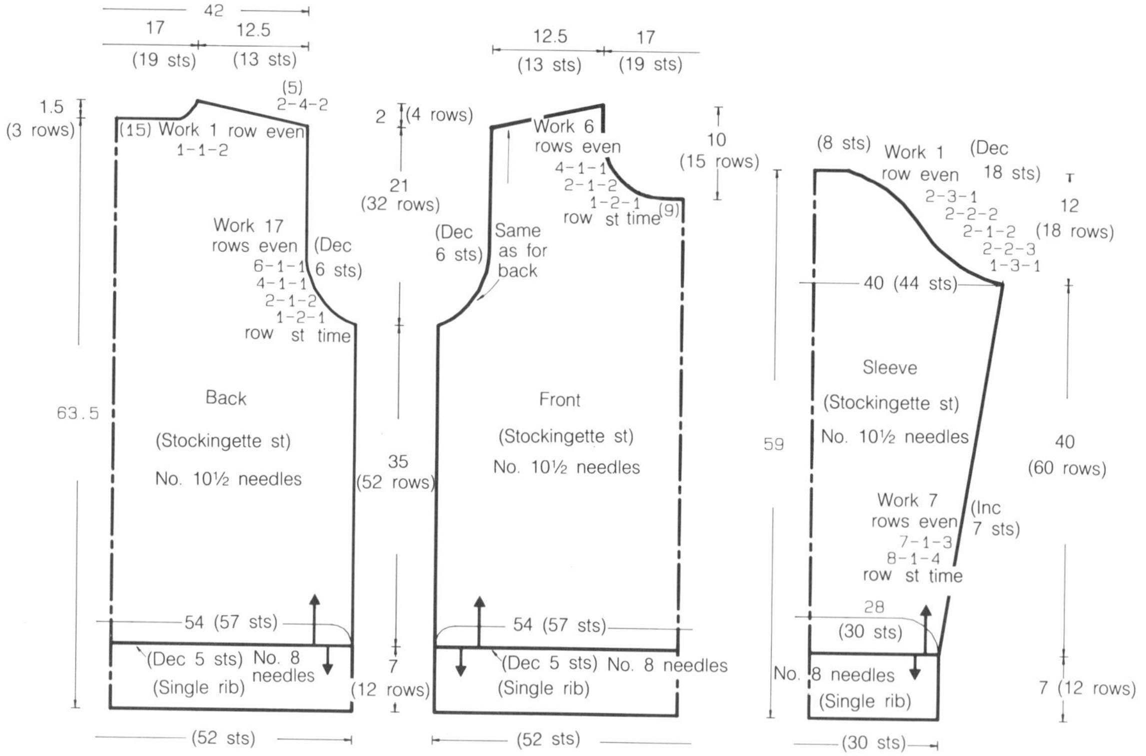

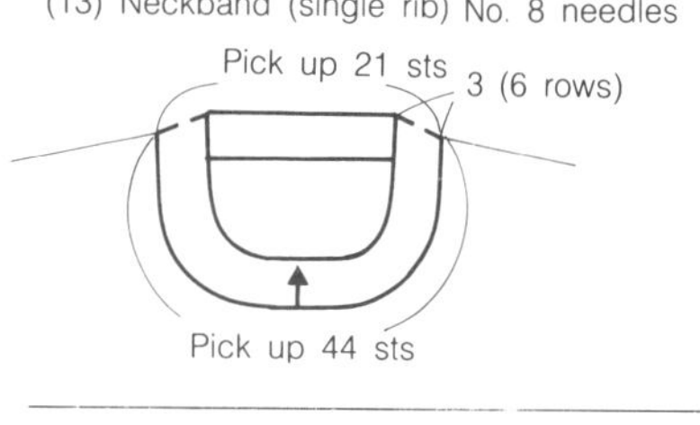

(13) Neckband (single rib) No. 8 needles

(14) Neckband (single rib) No. 8 needles

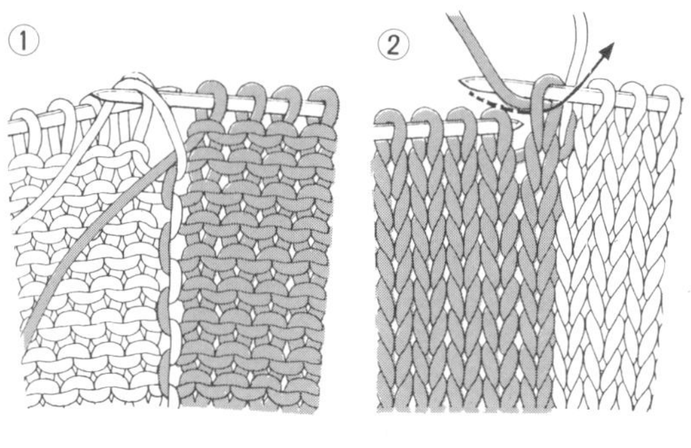

Changing yarn (joining vertical sections of color)

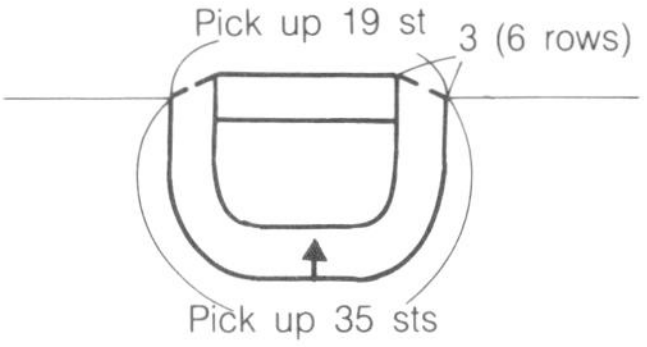

★ Shown on page 19.

MATERIALS: "Bulky Yarn" 210g yarn variegated color of gray, Turkish blue, gold, violet, pink, etc. 70g each of yarn variegated color of gray, orange, Turkish blue, gold, violet, etc., gray, purple, orange, gold, pink, etc. and gray, blue, dark blue, green, etc. 70g navy blue, 60g red, and 50g each of dark blue and blue.

NEEDLES: Knitting needles No. 10½ and No. 8.

SIZES: Bust ... 100cm. Length ... 57cm. Center of neck to wrist measurement ... 78cm.

GAUGE: 11 sts and 16 rows in 10cm square over pattern.

DIRECTIONS: Work pattern joining vertical sections of color, referring to the basic method of changing color on opposite page.

Color
A... Yarn variegated color of gray, Turkish blue, gold, violet, pink, etc.
B... Yarn variegated color of gray, orange, Turkish blue, gold, violet, etc.
C... Yarn variegated color of gray, purple, orange, gold, pink, etc.
D... Yarn variegated color of gray, blue, dark blue, green, etc.
A:... Red
B:... Dark blue
C:... Blue
D:... Navy blue

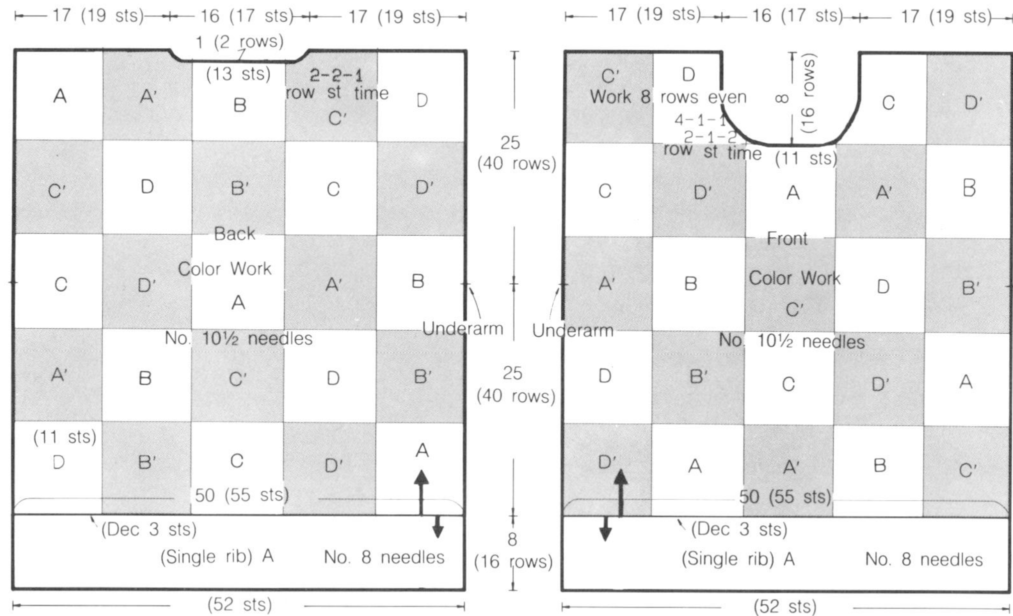

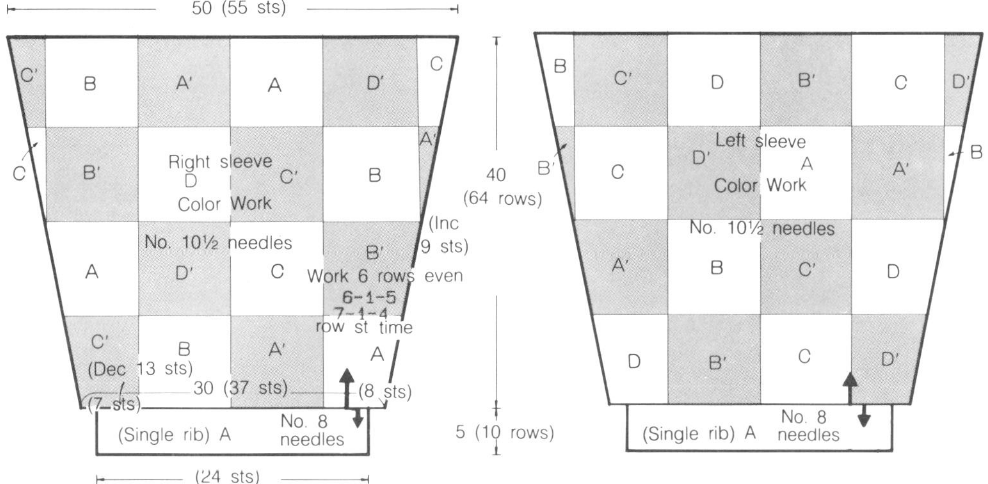

⑮ Crisp good looks will make
favorite for outdoors.
★ Knit with "Bulky Yarn"
★ Directions on page 24.
⑯ Nordic design inspires
some woman's pullover.
★ Knit with "Bulky Yarn"
★ Directions on page 25.

★ Shown on page 22.

MATERIALS: "Bulky Yarn" 270g dark brown, 230g pale gray, 110g grayish green, 50g sky gray, and 40g grayish rose.

NEEDLES: Knitting needles No. 8 and No. 7.

SIZES: Chest ... 106cm. Width across back measurement ... 42cm. Length ... 64cm. Outside sleeve ... 61cm.

GAUGE: 14 sts and 18 rows in 10cm square over color work.

DIRECTIONS: Referring to the way to work color on page 74, take the yarn not in use across the back of work. It is important to cross the yarns in the same direction at each color change and to pull the yarns equally.

Body: Make ch sts with another yarn, using crochet hook at the bottom, and transfer sts from wrong side of ch to No. 8 needle. Work rows even up to row 58, and start to shape armholes. Bind off sts at the beginning of row alternately to decrease over 2 sts. Work remaining sts to shape shoulder slope, referring to the basic method on page 74.

Sleeve: Lift loop lying 1 st inside both ends of previous row to increase sts for shaping sleeves.

Finishing: Join shoulder seam inside out working sl st with crochet hook, then work neckband circularly.

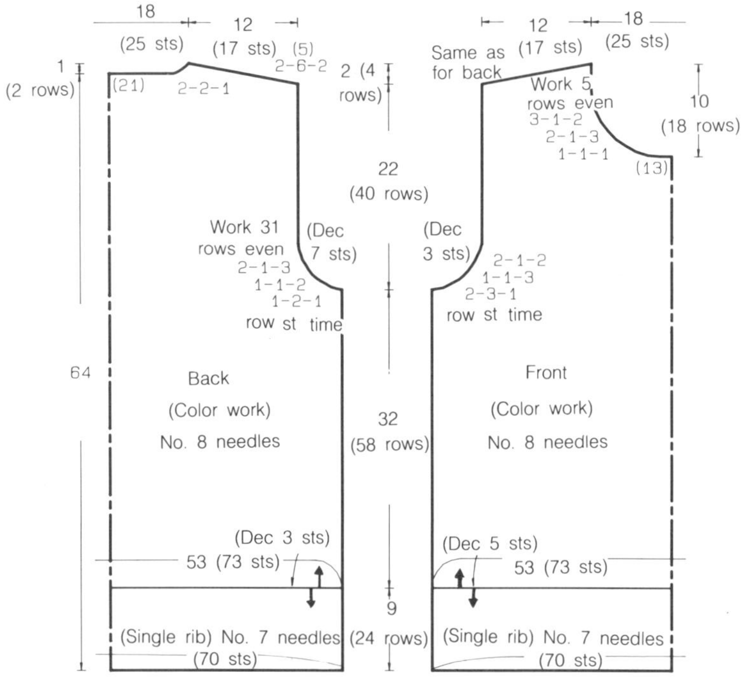

Schematics

Back (Color work) No. 8 needles — (Single rib) No. 7 needles

- 18 (25 sts), 12 (17 sts), (5), 2-6-2, 2 (4 rows)
- (21), 2-2-1
- 1 (2 rows)
- 64
- Work 31 rows even 2-1-3 1-1-2 1-2-1 row st time (Dec 7 sts)
- 22 (40 rows)
- 53 (73 sts) (Dec 3 sts)
- (70 sts)

Front (Color work) No. 8 needles — (Single rib) No. 7 needles

- Same as for back
- 12 (17 sts), 18 (25 sts)
- Work 5 rows even 3-1-2 2-1-3 1-1-1
- 10 (18 rows), (13)
- (Dec 3 sts) 2-1-2 1-1-3 2-3-1 row st time
- 32 (58 rows)
- 9 (24 rows)
- 53 (73 sts) (Dec 5 sts)
- (70 sts)

Color work

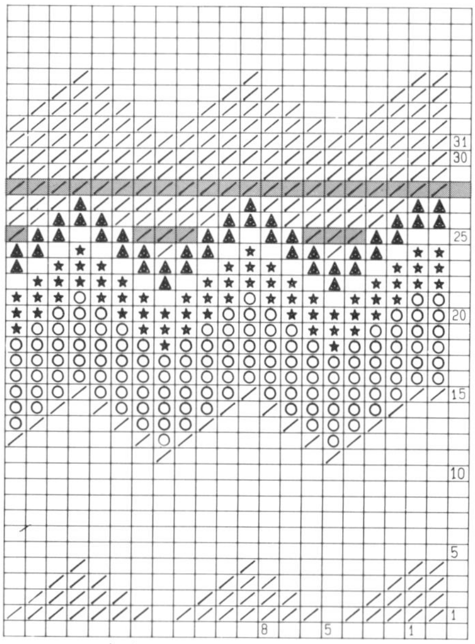

Color chart
- ⚠ ...Grayish rose
- ☆ ...Sky gray
- ○ ...Grayish green
- ╱ ...Dark brown
- ☐ ...Pale gray

▨ ... purl st

Sleeve (Color work) No. 8 needles

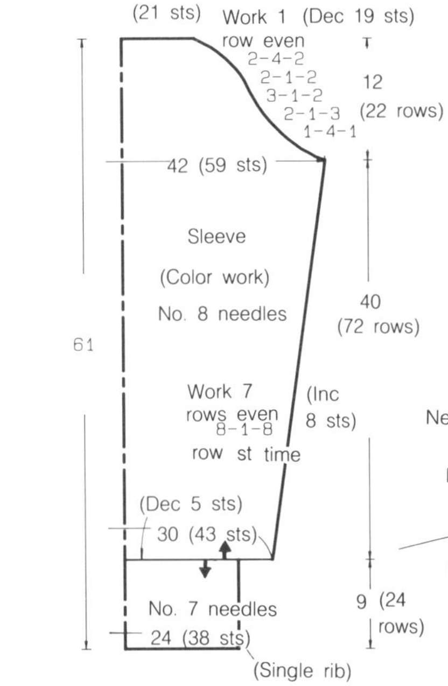

- (21 sts), Work 1 row even (Dec 19 sts) 2-4-2 2-1-2 3-1-2 2-1-3 1-4-1
- 12 (22 rows)
- 42 (59 sts)
- 61
- 40 (72 rows)
- Work 7 rows even 8-1-8 row st time (Inc 8 sts)
- 30 (43 sts) (Dec 5 sts)
- No. 7 needles
- 24 (38 sts) (Single rib)
- 9 (24 rows)

Neckband (single rib) Dark brown No. 7 needles

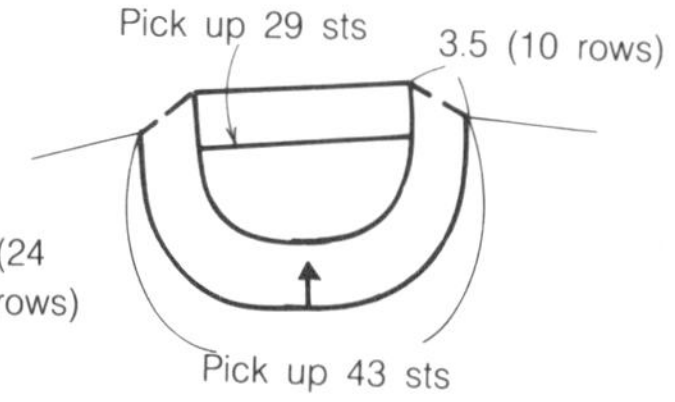

- Pick up 29 sts
- 3.5 (10 rows)
- Pick up 43 sts

Color chart
- ⚠ ...Grayish rose
- • ...Gold
- ☆ ...Sky gray
- ╱ ...Dark brown
- ○ ...Grayish green
- ☐ ...Pale gray

Neckband (single rib) No. 7 needles   Dark brown

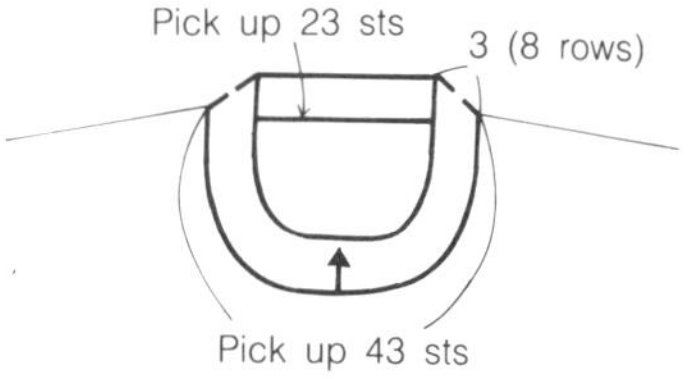

- Pick up 23 sts
- 3 (8 rows)
- Pick up 43 sts

Color work A

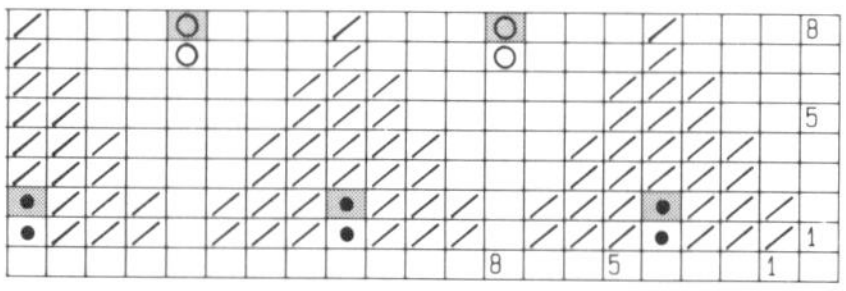

MATERIALS: "Bulky Yarn" 240g pale gray, 210g dark brown, 35g grayish green, 30g each of sky gray, gold, and 10g grayish rose.

NEEDLES: Knitting needles No. 8 and No. 7.

SIZES: Bust ... 100cm. Width across back measurement ... 38cm. Length ... 56.5cm. Outside sleeve ... 54cm.

GAUGE: 14 sts and 18 rows in 10cm square over stockingette st and color work.

DIRECTIONS: Referring to the basic method of color work on page 74, take yarn not in use across the back of work. It is important to cross the yarns in the same direction at each color change and to pull the yarns equally.

Body: Make ch sts with another yarn using crochet hook, and transfer sts from wrong side of ch to No. 8 needles. Color work A is shown on right bottom of opposite page. Work sts referring to chart.

Sleeve: Increase sts to shape sleeve, lifting loop lying 1 st inside both ends of previous row.

Finishing: Join shoulder seam inside out, working sl st with crochet hook; then work neckband circularly. Sew side and sleeve seams with covercasting stitch. Pin sleeve neatly in body inside out and join with sl st.

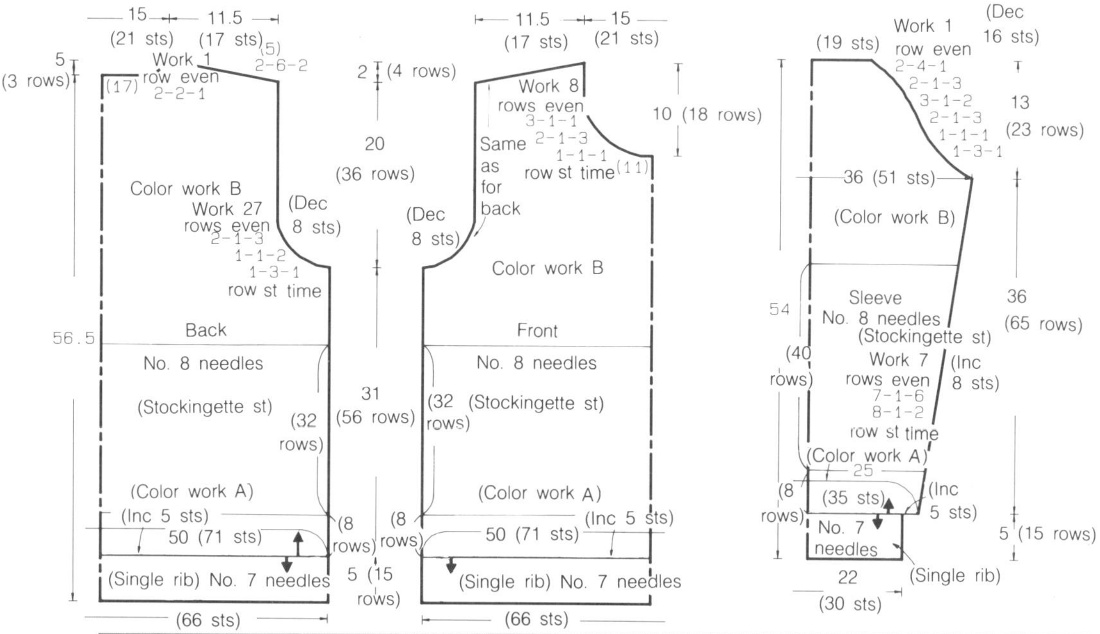

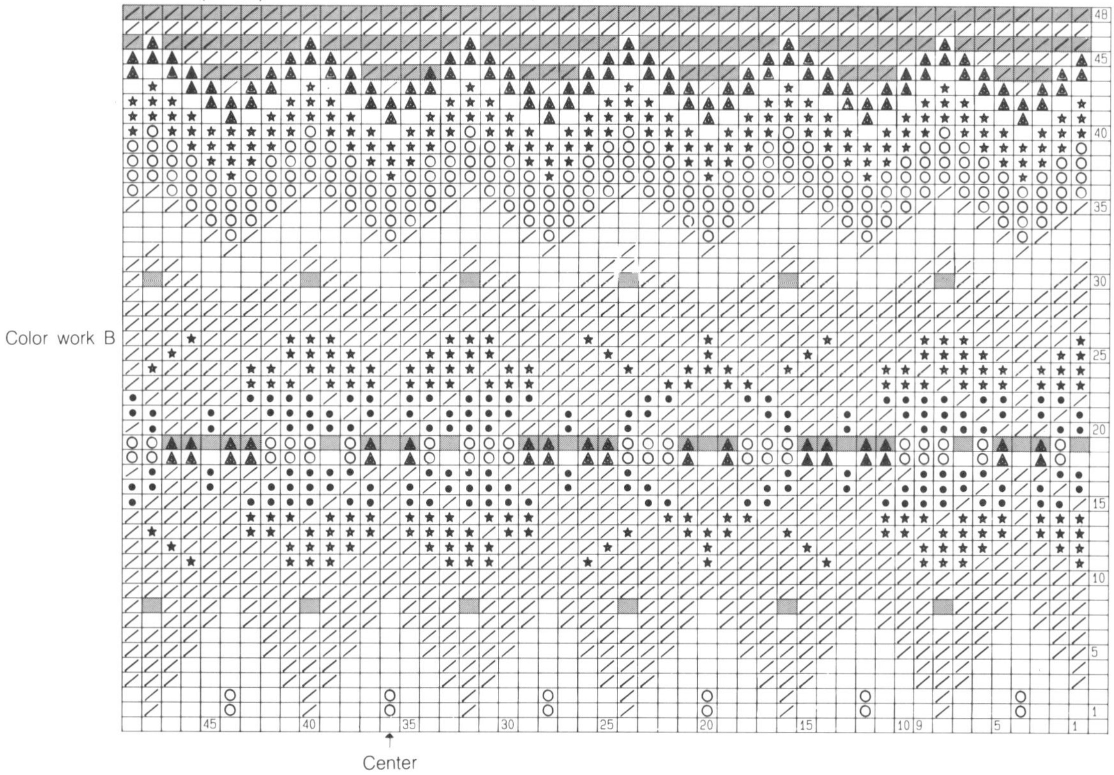

★ **Shown on page 23.**

⑰ Here's a smart-looking pullover for
sophisticated relaxation.
★ "Bulky Yarn"
★ Directions on page 28.
⑱ Whether you're schussing or a
spectator, you'll look good outdoors
in this.
★ "Bulky Yarn"
★ Directions on page 29.
17

18

★ **Shown on page 26.**

MATERIALS: "Bulky Yarn" 470g dark brown and 170g off-white.
NEEDLES: Knitting yarn No. 9 and No. 7.
SIZES: Bust ... 100cm. Length ... 58cm. Center of neck to wrist measurement ... 72.5cm.
GAUGE: 14 sts and 23 rows in 10cm square over pattern. 14 sts and 19 rows in 10cm square over stockingette st.
DIRECTIONS: Make ch sts with another yarn using crochet hook, and transfer sts from wrong side of ch to No. 9 needle. Work pattern showing the sign ... with slip st and ... with raise st, referring to diagram on opposite page. Work pattern of body up to row 52, and work 8 rows in stockingette st

with dark brown. Bind off 4 sts at under-arms, and decrease remaining sts 2 stockingette sts on both ends to shape raglan armholes. Increase sts to shape sleeves, lifting loop lying 2 sts inside both ends of previous row. Decrease as for body leaving 2 stockingette sts on both ends. After doing body and sleeves, unfasten ch st and pick up sts from row 1, then start single rib. See page 74 on the finishing of single rib. Sew raglan armholes with overcasting st, picking up loops lying 1 st inside raglan line, then work 84 sts for neckband circularly. Sew side and sleeve seams with overcasting sts on every row.

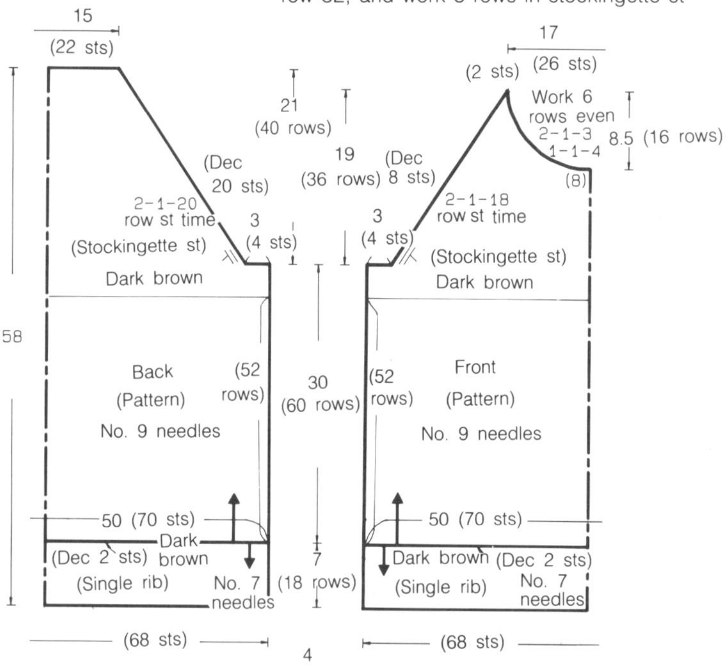

Pattern chart (for both men's and women's)

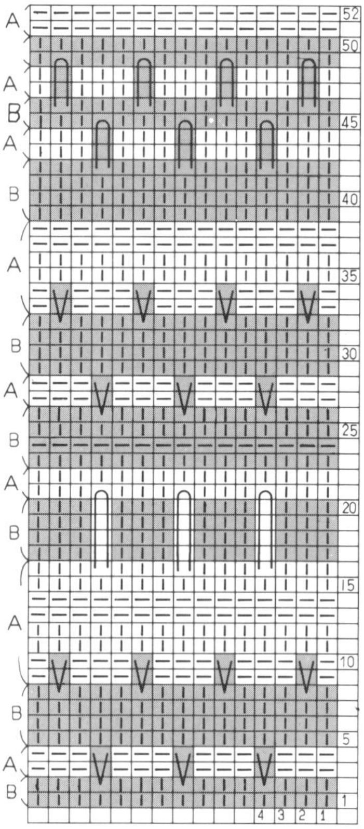

Color
A ... off-white
B ... dark-brown

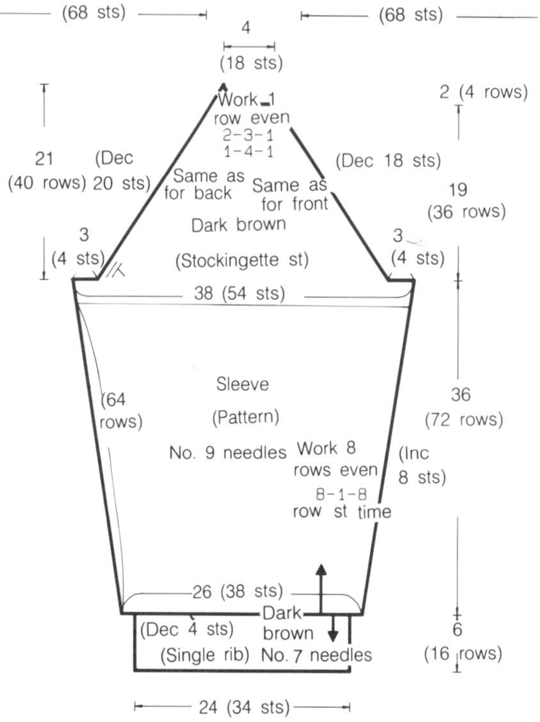

Neckband (single rib) No. 7 needles Off-white

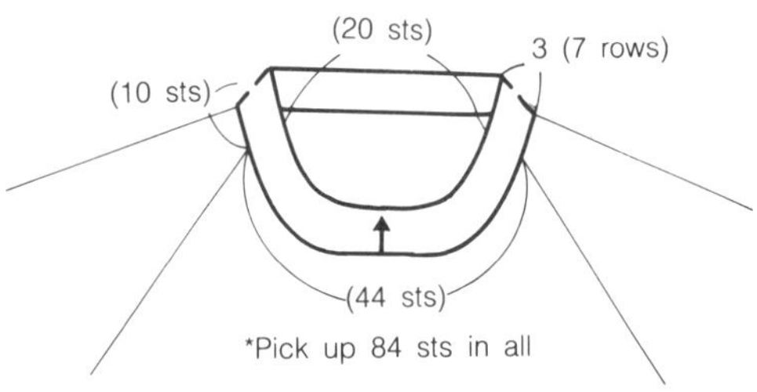

*Pick up 84 sts in all

18

★ **Shown on page 27.**

MATERIALS: "Bulky Yarn" 500g dark brown, 380g off-white.

NEEDLES: Knitting needles No. 9 and No. 7.

SIZES: Chest ... 104cm. Length ... 63.5cm. Center of neck to wrist measurement ... 83cm.

GAUGE: 14 sts and 23 rows in 10cm square over pattern.

DIRECTIONS: Make ch st with another yarn using crochet hook, and transfer sts from wrong side of ch to No. 9 needle.

Men's and women's patterns are in common, as shown on opposite page. Work 78 rows even up to underarm, and bind off 4 sts. Decrease these sts at the beginning of row; work the right side on the first row and the left side on the second row. Decrease sts leaving 2 stockingette sts on both ends to shape raglan armholes, and stand out 2 stockingette sts line after joining body and sleeve. Increase sts of sleeves lifting loop lying 2 sts inside both ends of previous row. Decrease as for body leaving 2 stockingette sts on both ends; then stand out 2 stockingette sts on sleeve seam. Sew raglan armholes with overcasting st, pick up 89 sts for neckband and work rib circularly. See page 74 on finishing the rib.

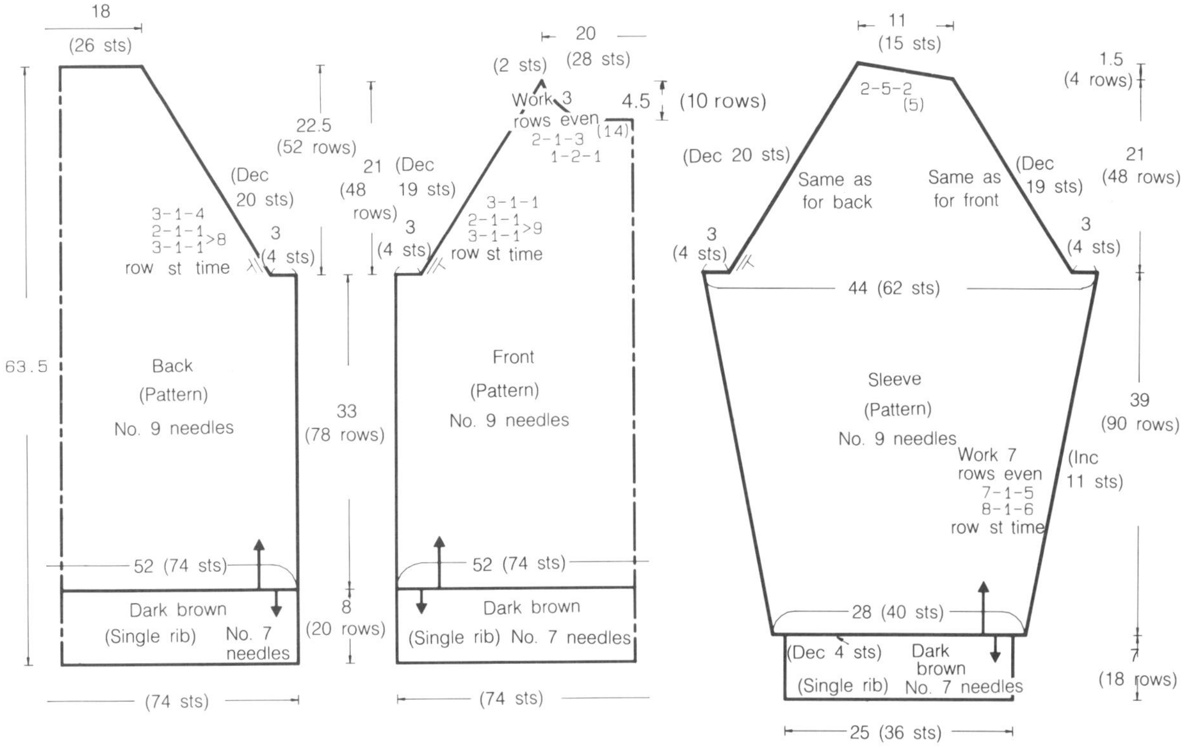

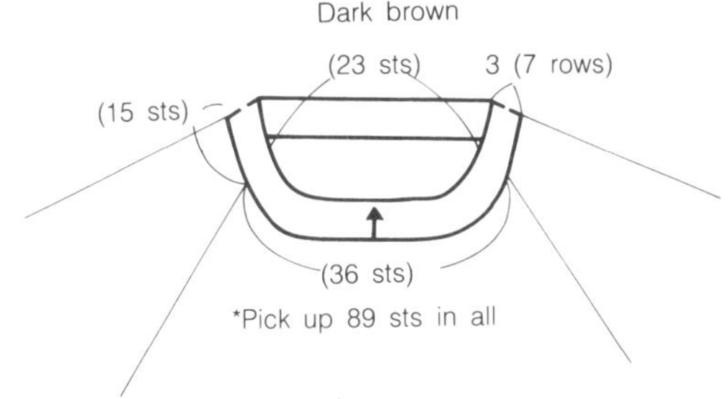

Neckband (single rib) No. 7 needles
Dark brown

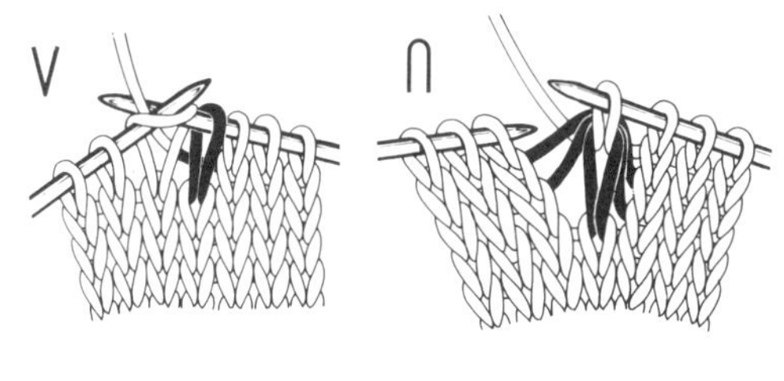

Stadium breeze

⑲ A natural-colored yarn plays up
this sensational pattern.
★ **Knit with "Bulky Yarn"**
★ **Directions on page 32.**
⑳ This is easy to knit, but oh-so-
smart and good-looking to wear.
★ **Knit with "Bulky Yarn"**
★ **Directions on page 33.**

20

★ **Shown on page 30.**

MATERIALS: "Bulky Yarn" 630g off-white.
NEEDLES: Knitting needles No. 4–5

SIZES: Bust ... 96cm. Length ... 55cm. Center of neck to wrist measurement ... 70cm.
GAUGE: 20 sts and 32 rows in 10cm square over pattern.
DIRECTIONS: Make ch sts with another yarn using crochet hook and transfer sts from wrong side of ch to No. 4–5 needle to start body and sleeves. Pay attention to the start of pattern for front, back, and sleeves. Continue sts even up to neckline, marking the points of underarm. To shape neck, place remaining center sts on holder, and work right and left separately. Bind off sts at the beginning of rows alternately to decrease over 2 sts. Increase sts of sleeves lifting loop lying 1 st inside both ends of previous row. After making body and sleeves, unfasten the foundation ch and pick up sts, then work single rib toward opposite direction. Join shoulder seam inside out with sl st using crochet hook, and work neckband circularly. Place sleeve inside out on body, and join neatly with sl st. Sew sleeve and side seam with overcasting st.

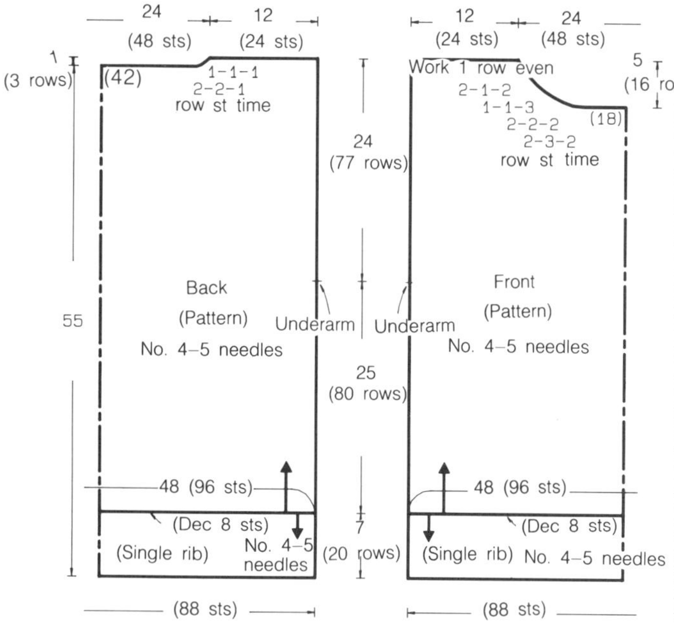

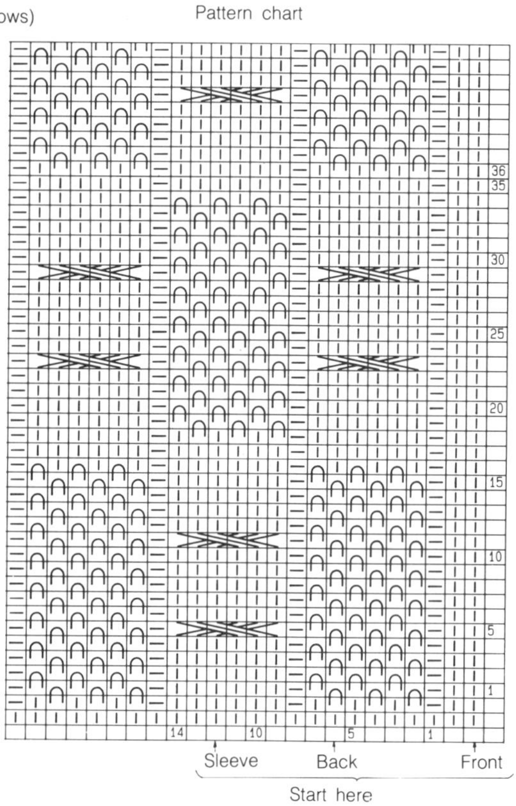

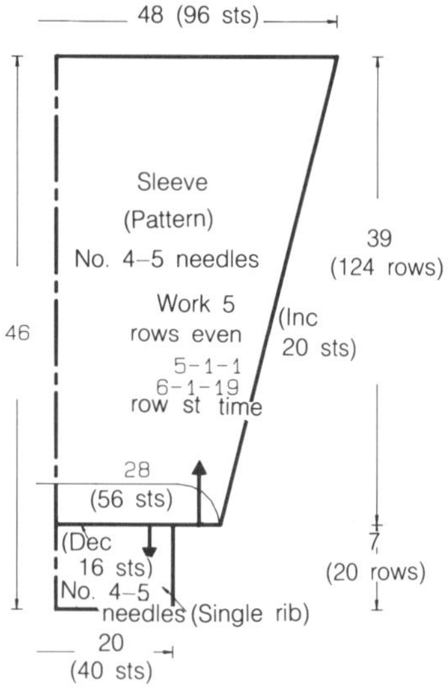

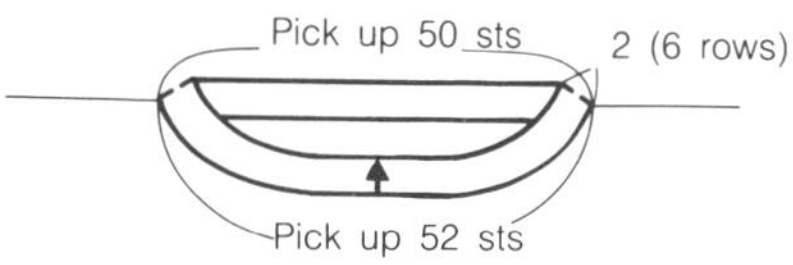

★ Shown on page 31.

MATERIALS: "Bulky Yarn" 650g off-white (223).

NEEDLES: Knitting needles No. 8 and No. 6.

SIZES: Bust ... 98cm. Length ... 56.5cm. Center of neck to wrist measurement ... 70cm.

GAUGE: 15.5 sts and 26 rows in 10cm square over pattern.

DIRECTIONS: Make ch sts with another yarn using crochet hook and transfer sts from wrong side of ch to No. 8 needles.

Back and front: Work 68 rows even up to underarms and bind off 5 sts. Decrease these sts at the beginning of row; work

left side at the following row on back side. Work even until neckline, and place remaining center sts on holder. Work right and left separately. Bind off sts at the beginning of rows to decrease over 2 sts.

Sleeve: Increase sts, lifting loop lying 1 st inside both ends of previous row to shape sleeve. Work in pattern to desired rows, and bind off.

Finishing: Join shoulder seams inside out, working sl st with crochet hook. Pick up 78 sts from neckline of body and work single rib 9 rows circularly. Set sleeve neatly in body inserting hook 1 st inside edge with sl st. Join underarms at the points designated by ⊙ with overcasting st. See page 74 on finishing single rib.

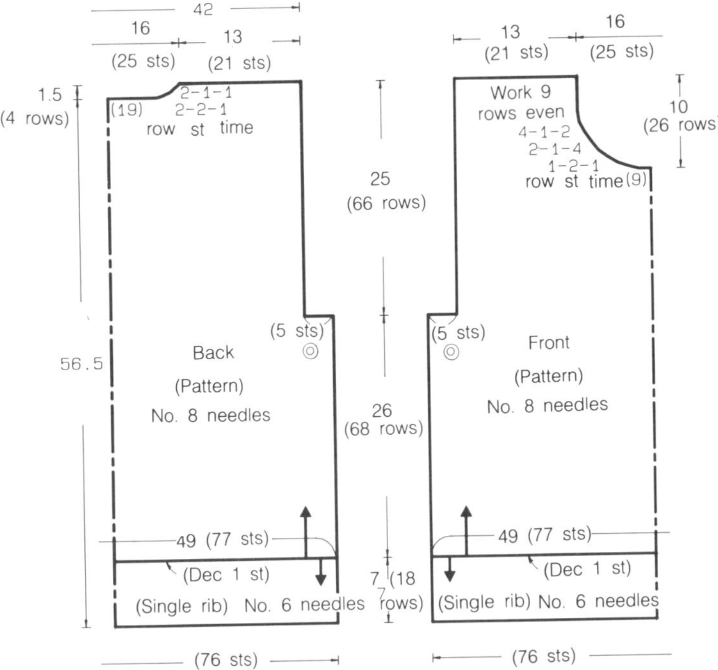

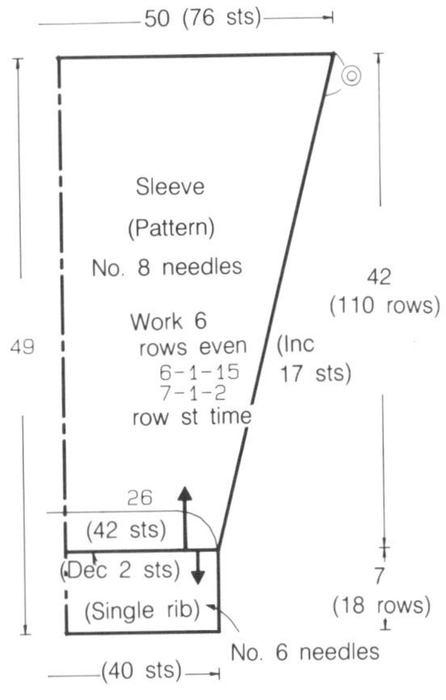

Pattern chart

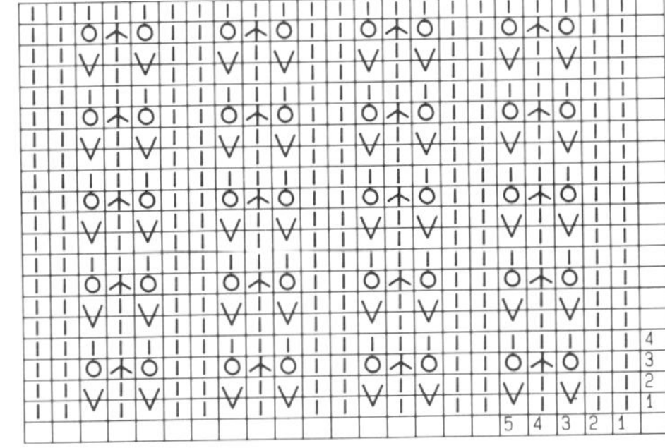

Neckband (single rib) No. 6 needles

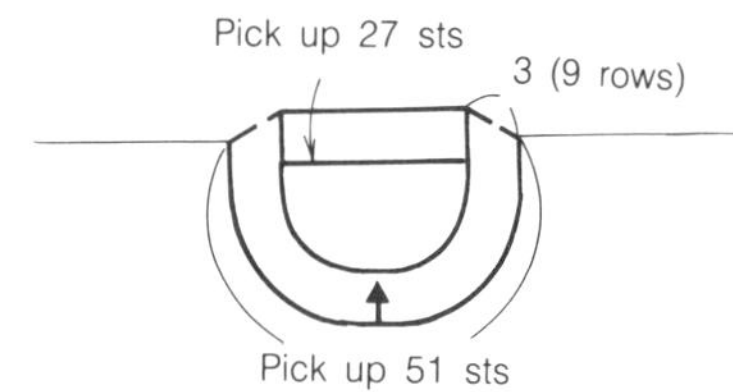

21

㉑ Deep-toned geometrics—a pleasure
to knit as well as wear.
★ **Knit with "Bulky Yarn"**
★ **Directions on page 36.**
㉒ This simple zigzag pattern packs a
lot of style.
★ **Knit with "Bulky Yarn"**
★ **Directions on page 37.**

35

★ **Shown on page 24.**

MATERIALS: "Bulky Yarn" 350g purplish blue and 250g dark gray.

NEEDLES: Knitting needles No. 9 and No. 6.

SIZES: Bust ... 96cm. Length ... 56cm. Center of neck to wrist measurement ... 57cm.

GAUGE: 8 sts and 15 rows in 8cm square over each mosaic.

DIRECTIONS: Work back and front in same manner. Work in numerical order shown on chart. Make triangular pieces for every side and a square piece for the inside, referring to chart below and on page 73. Cast on 2 sts at left bottom and knit 2 rows at first. Turn and increase left 1 st on right side, as shown below. Repeat this 7 times, and complete 16 sts and 9 rows of triangular piece. Place 8 sts on holder, and 1 st remain on needle, continuing to next triangle. Turn and make triangle in same way. Start from right side on second step. Work 2 sts together every 2 rows, joining with each remaining st of piece 6. Pick up 8 sts from each 2 rows of piece 6, and work piece 8 in the same manner. Knit until row 15; then pick up 8 sts from piece 5 to form piece 9. Repeat this work to complete the body and sleeves. Pick up the required number of sts from the neck, lower border, and wrist with sl st using crochet hook and work rib. Sew shoulder seams overlapping each rib band.

Back and front (pattern chart) No. 9 needles

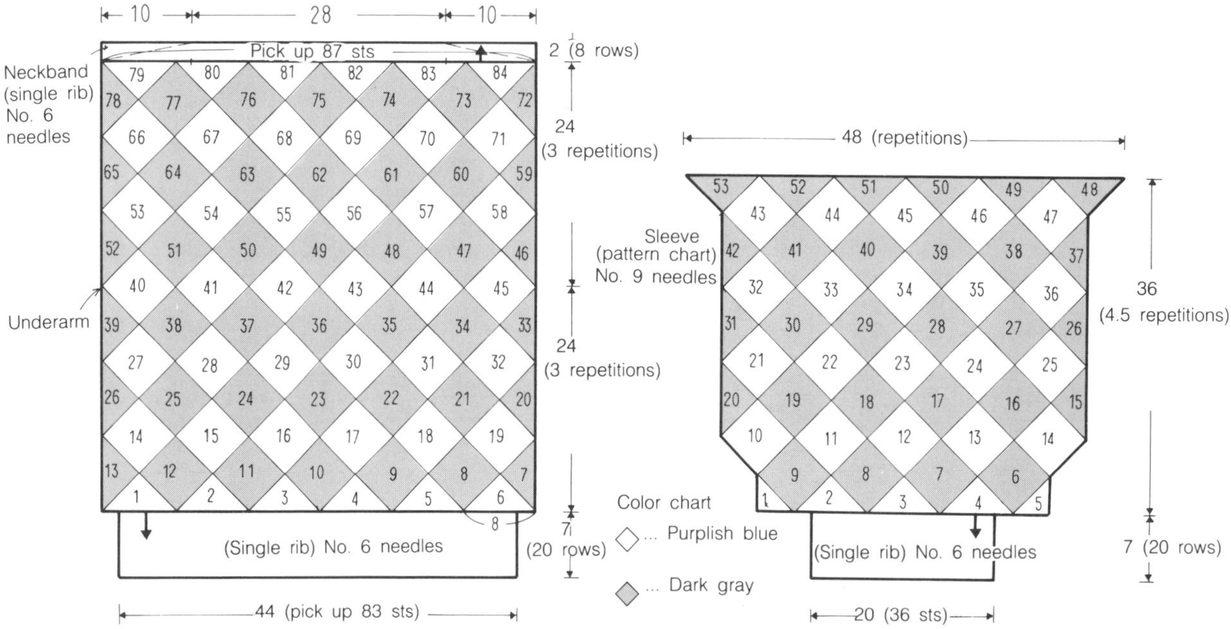

Color chart
◇ ... Purplish blue
◆ ... Dark gray

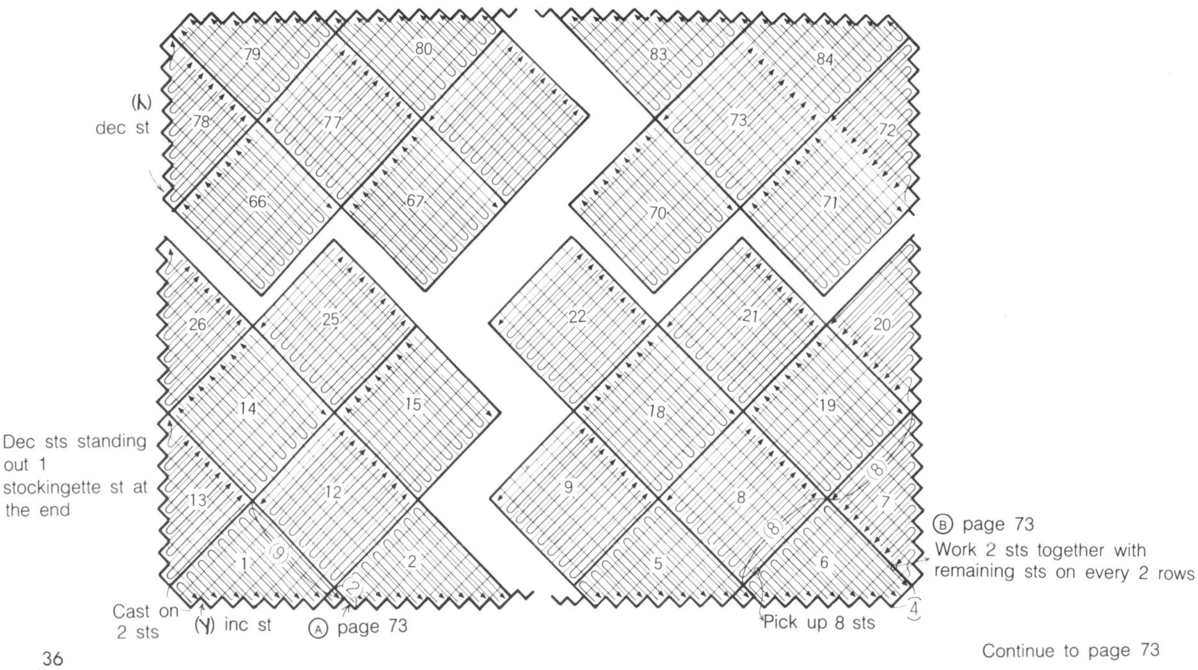

Dec sts standing out 1 stockingette st at the end

Ⓑ page 73
Work 2 sts together with remaining sts on every 2 rows

Continue to page 73

★ Shown on page 35.

MATERIALS: "Bulky Yarn" 530g smoky blue.

NEEDLES: Knitting needles No. 7. Crochet hook No. 4–5.

SIZES: Bust ... 96cm. Length ... 50cm. Center of neck to wrist measurement ... 67cm.

GAUGE: 20 sts and 23 rows in 10cm square over pattern.

DIRECTIONS: Start body and sleeves casting on required number of sts. These sts are counted as row 1.

Back and front: Work 64 rows even until underarm, and bind off 6 sts. With binding off sts at the beginning of row, work left end on wrong side. Work rows even until neck-line. Place center 34 sts on holder, and work 2 rows separately to shape back neckline. Place center 16 sts on holder, and decrease right and left sts separately for front neck-line.

Sleeve: Increase sts for sleeves, lifting loop lying 1 st inside both ends of previous row. Work 104 rows and bind off.

Finishing: Join shoulder seams inside out with sl st using crochet hook, and work sc for neckband. Set sleeves neatly in body with sl st. Sew underarms of body and sleeves with overcasting sts.

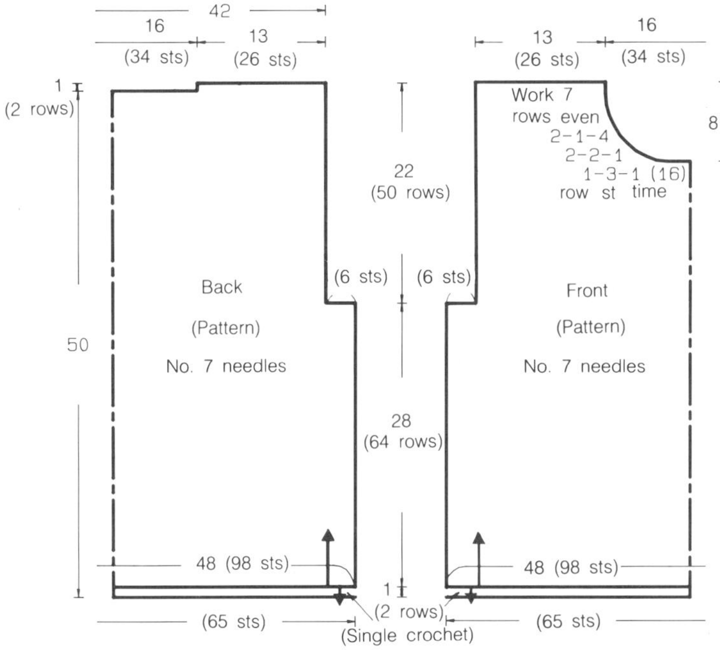

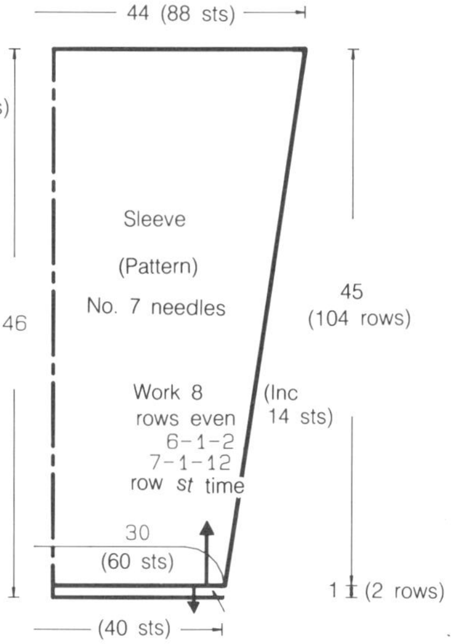

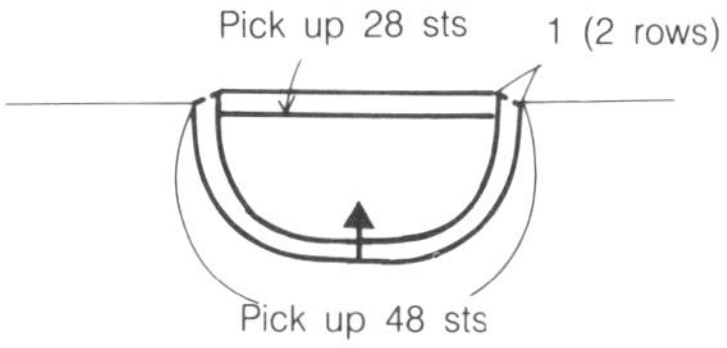

Inc st at both ends

Knit the first st

Neckband (sc) crochet hook No. 4–5

Pick up 28 sts 1 (2 rows)

Pick up 48 sts

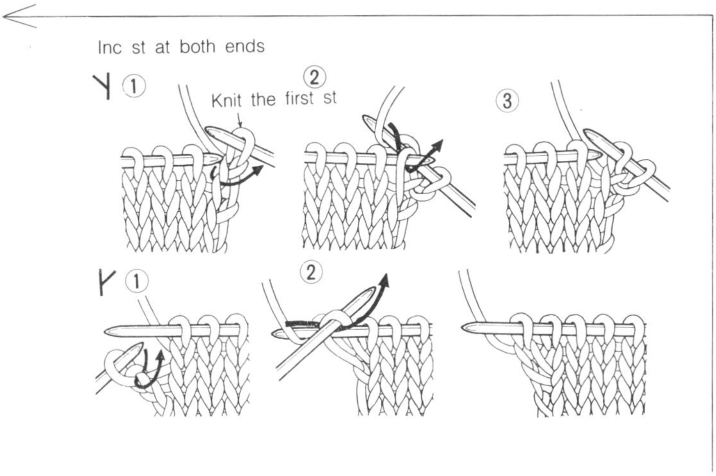

Pattern chart

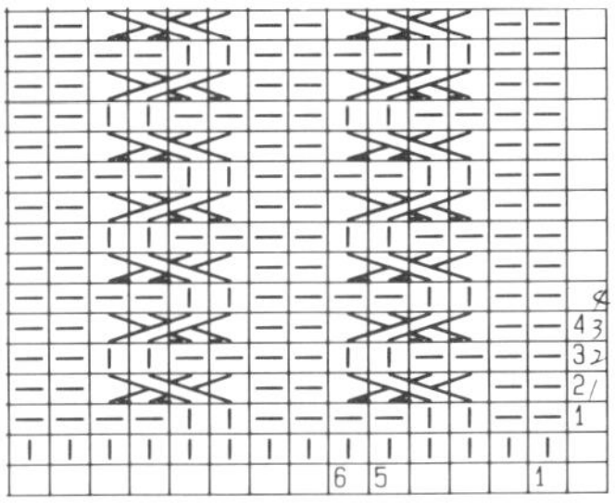

23

㉓ Mohair doubles the beauty of t... soft cable design.
★ **Knit with "Bulky Yarn"**
★ **Directions on page 40.**
㉔ A stylish coup—to which th... toned yarn contributes.
★ **Knit with "Bulky Yarn"**
★ **Directions on page 41.**

24

★ Shown on page 38.

MATERIALS: "Bulky Yarn" 380g dark blue.
NEEDLES: Knitting needles No. 9.
SIZES: Bust ... 96cm. Width across back measurement ... 36cm. Length ... 54.5cm. Outside sleeve ... 54cm.
GAUGE: 11 sts and 15 rows in 10cm square over reversed stockingette st.
DIRECTIONS: Make ch st with another yarn using crochet hook, and transfer sts from wrong side of ch to No. 9 needles.
Body: Work reversed stockingette st and pattern as shown below; be sure to work cable st symmetrically. Work 44 rows even up to underarm, then decrease sts to shape armholes. In case of decreasing over 2 sts,

bind off sts at the beginning of rows alternately. With remaining sts turn to shape shoulder seam, referring to diagram on page 74.
Sleeve: Increase sts of sleeves, lifting loop lying 1 st inside both ends of previous row. Decrease sts of cap at the beginning of alternate rows.
Finishing: Join shoulder seam inside out with sl st using crochet hook, and pick up 70 sts from neckline; then work 6 rows circularly. Pin sleeve neatly inside out on armhole of body and join with sl st.

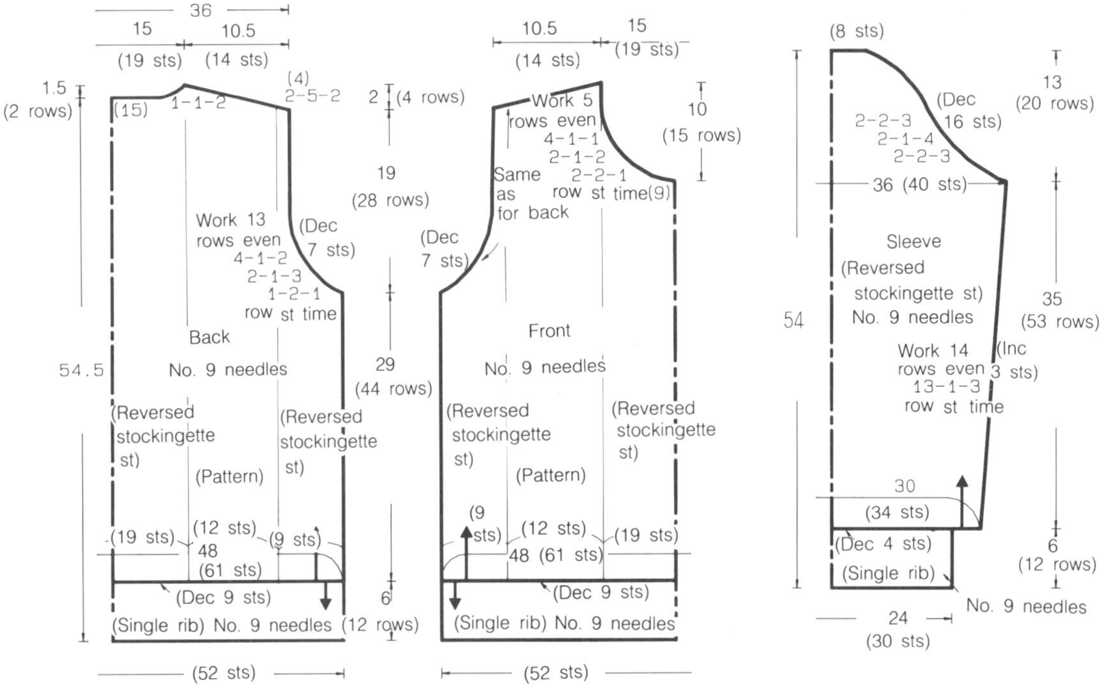

Pattern chart (right side)

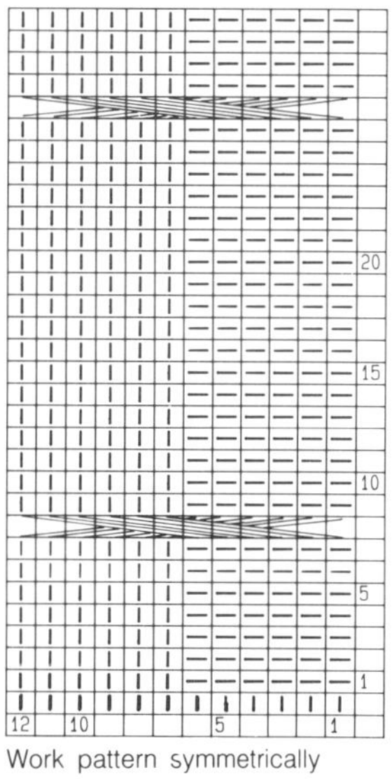

Work pattern symmetrically

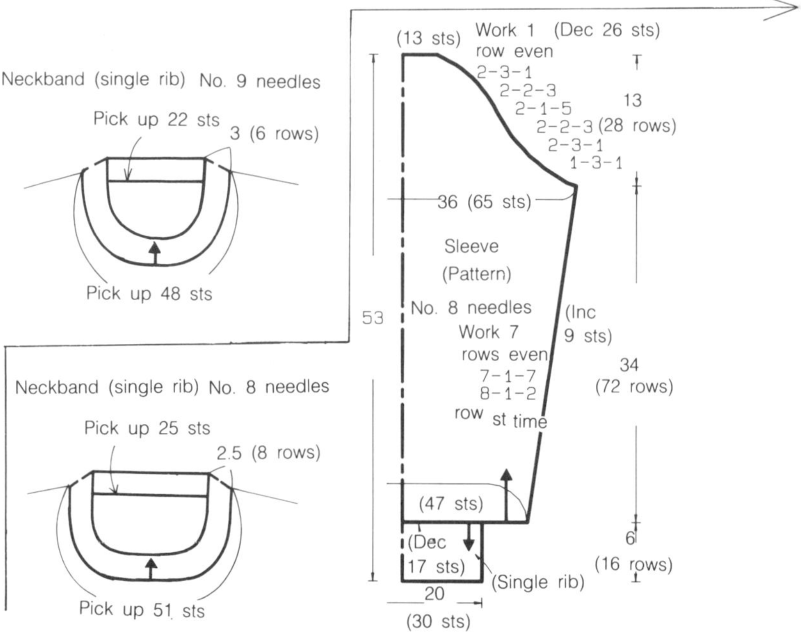

Neckband (single rib) No. 9 needles

Neckband (single rib) No. 8 needles

★ Shown on page 39.

MATERIALS: "Bulky Yarn" 570g off-white with variegated skeins of gray and silver gradation

NEEDLES: Knitting needles No. 8.

SIZES: Bust ... 96cm. Width across back measurement ... 36cm. Length ... 54.5cm. Outside sleeve ... 53cm.

GAUGE: 18 sts and 21 rows in 10cm square over pattern.

DIRECTIONS: Make ch sts with another yarn using crochet hook, and transfer sts from wrong side of ch to No. 8 needle to start body and sleeves.

Body: Work 60 rows even up to underarm, and decrease sts to shape armholes. In de-creasing over 2 sts, bind off sts at the begin-ning of rows; work the right end on the first row and the left end on the second row. See diagram on page 74 to shape shoulder seam with the remaining sts.

Sleeve: Increase sts, lifting loop lying 1 st inside both ends of previous row.

Finishing: Unfasten the foundation ch and pick up sts to work rib for lower border and wrist toward opposite ends. (See page 74 on finishing single rib.) Join shoulder seam inside out with sl st using crochet hook. Pick up 76 sts from neckline, and work 8 rows circularly. Sew side and sleeve seam with overcasting st. Set sleeves neatly inside out in body with sl st.

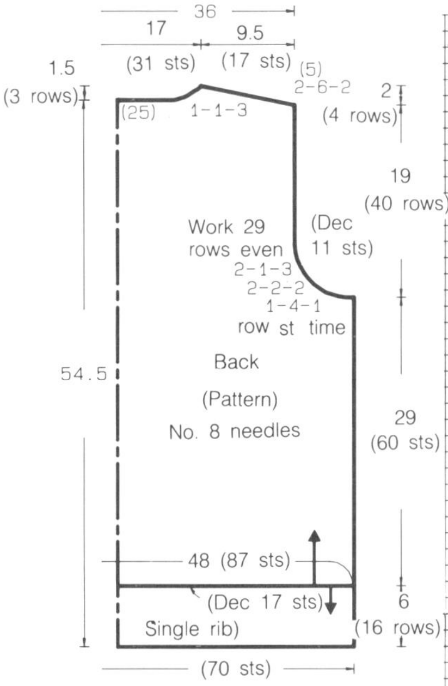

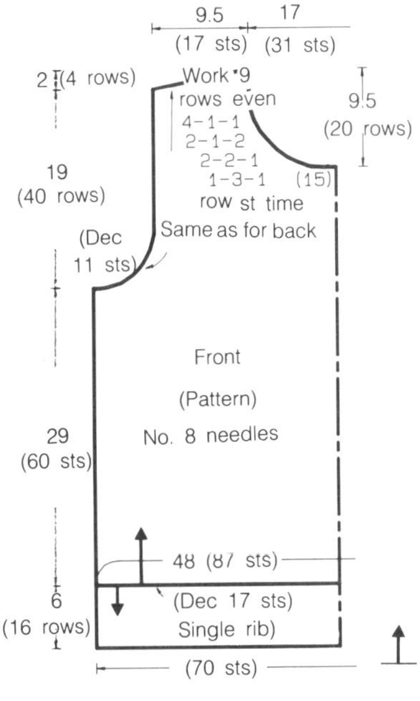

Pattern chart   ☐ = purl st

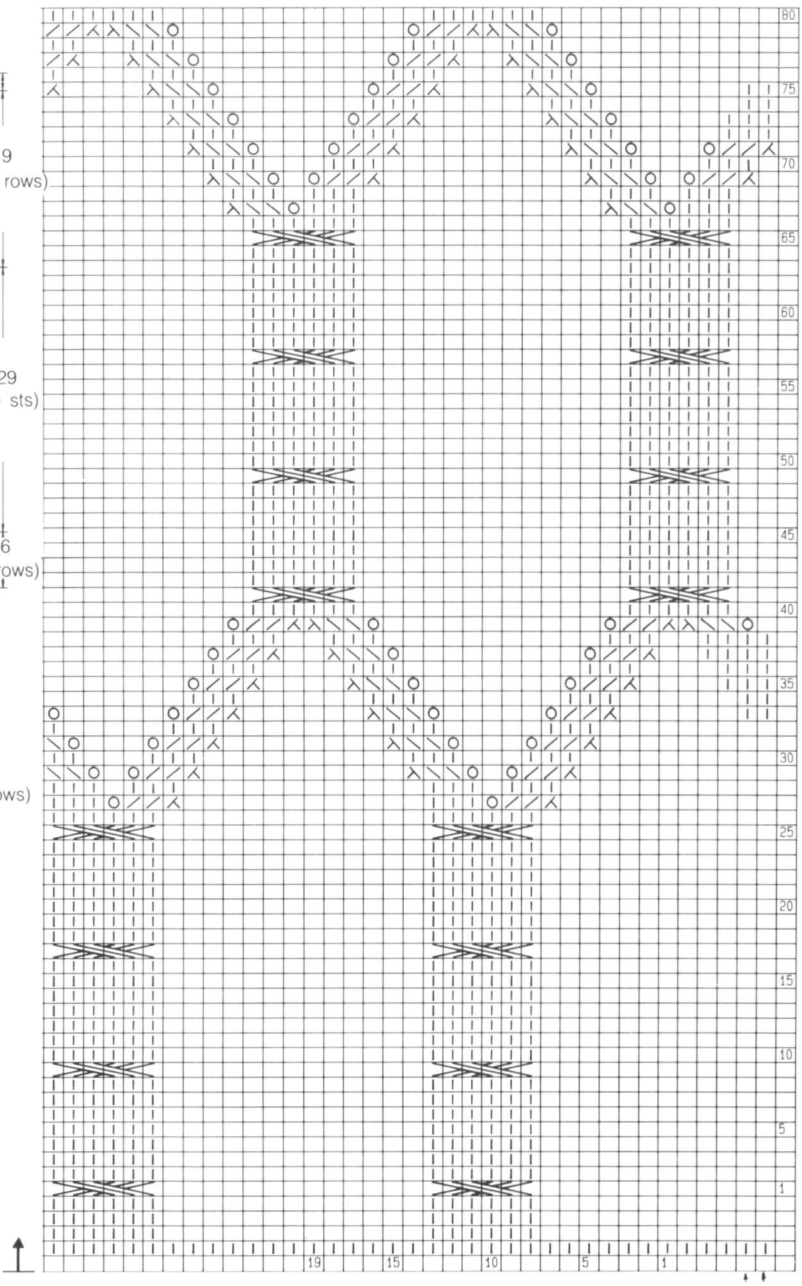

㉕ Here's a triumph of cables and
four-color stripes.
★ Knit with "Bulky Yarn"
★ Directions on page 44.
25

42

㉖ This wonderfully feminine leaf
design looks chic in olive.
★ Knit with "Bulky Yarn"
★ Directions on page 45.

26

★ **Shown on page 42.**

MATERIALS: "Bulky Yarn" 160g olive green and 130g each of blue, blue-green, and mustard.

NEEDLES: Knitting needles No. 6 and No. 4–5.

SIZES: Bust ... 96cm. Width across back measurement ... 36cm. Length ... 53.5cm. Outside sleeve ... 52.5cm.

GAUGE: 22 sts and 28 rows in 10cm square over pattern.

DIRECTIONS: Make ch st with another yarn using crochet hook, and transfer sts from wrong side of ch to No. 6 needle. Start from color a (blue) on body and color d (blue-green) on sleeves; then repeat 4 colors every 14 rows.

Body: In decreasing over 2 sts, bind off sts at the beginning of rows alternately to shape armholes. See diagram on page 74 the method of shaping shoulder seam.

Sleeve: Increase sts to shape sleeve, lifting loop lying 1 st inside both ends of previous row.

Finishing: Unfasten the foundation ch and pick up st to work rib for body and wrist toward opposite end. Join shoulder seam with sl st using crochet hook. Pick up 96 sts from neck-line, and work 18 rows with color c (olive green) circularly. Pin sleeves neatly inside out in body and join with sl st.

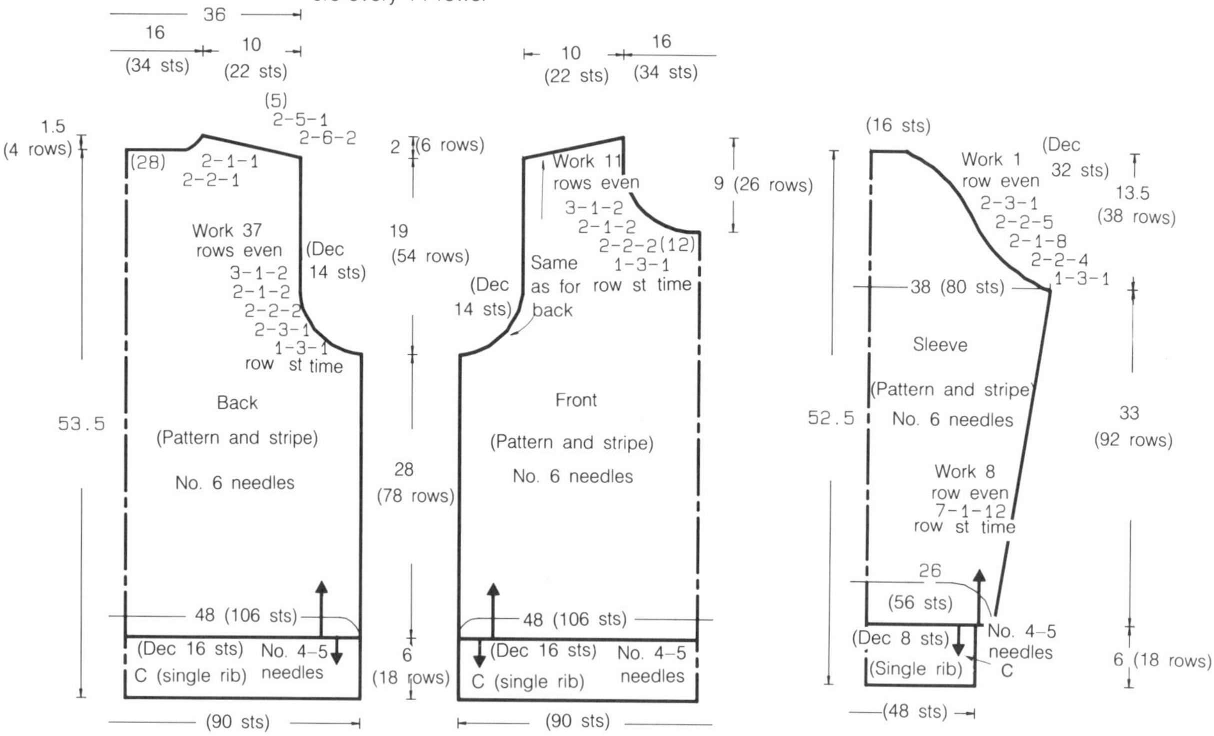

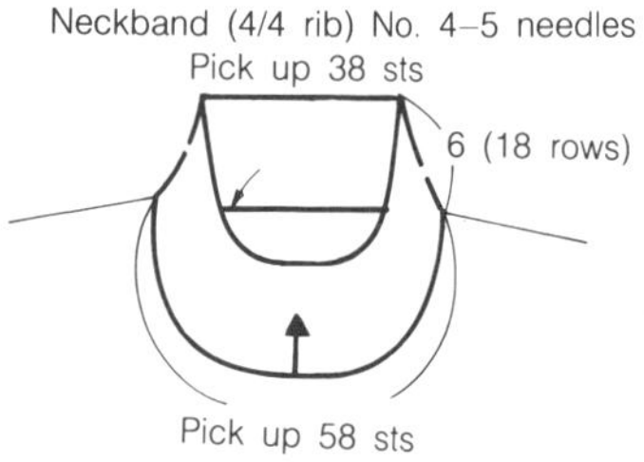

Pattern chart

Color chart

Repeat:
- d — Blue-green / sleeve
- c — Olive green
- b — Mustard
- a — Blue / body

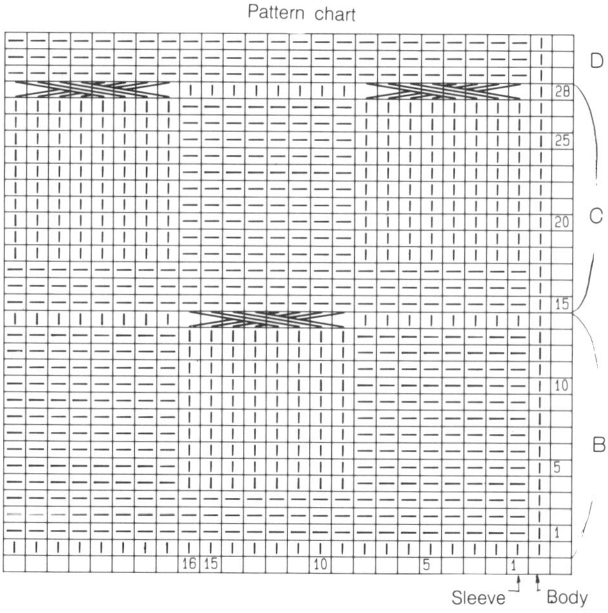

Neckband (4/4 rib) No. 4–5 needles
Pick up 38 sts
6 (18 rows)
Pick up 58 sts

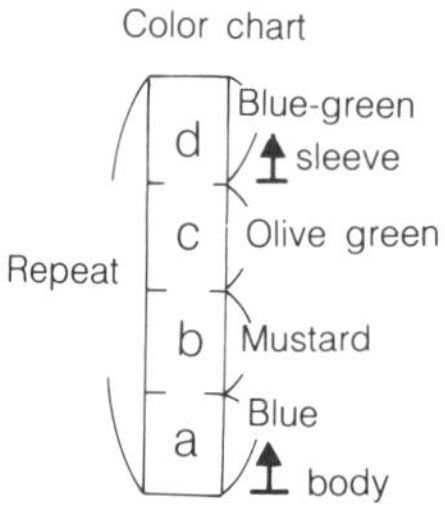

MATERIALS: "Bulky Yarn" 500g olive green.
NEEDLES: Knitting needles No. 7 and No. 6.
SIZES: Bust ... 96cm. Width cross back measurement ... 36cm. Length ... 54.5cm. Outside sleeve ... 53cm.
GAUGE: 15 sts and 22 rows in 10cm square over pattern.
DIRECTION: Make ch st with another yarn using crochet hook, and transfer sts from wrong side of ch to No. 7 needle to start body and sleeves. Do not miss the starting point of pattern.
Body: Work 60 rows even up to underarm.

★ **Shown on page 43.**

In decreasing over 2 sts, bind off sts at the beginning of rows alternately. See diagram of page 74 on working remaining sts to shape shoulder slope.
Sleeve: Increase sts to shape shoulder, lifting loop lying 1 st inside both ends of previous row.
Finishing: Work single rib for body and sleeves. Unfasten the foundation ch, and pick up sts from sinker loop of the first row. Join shoulder seam inside out with sl st using crochet hook and work neckband. Pick up 76 sts from neckline and work 6 rows circularly. Sew side and sleeve seam with overcasting st. Pin sleeves inside out in body and join neatly with sl st.

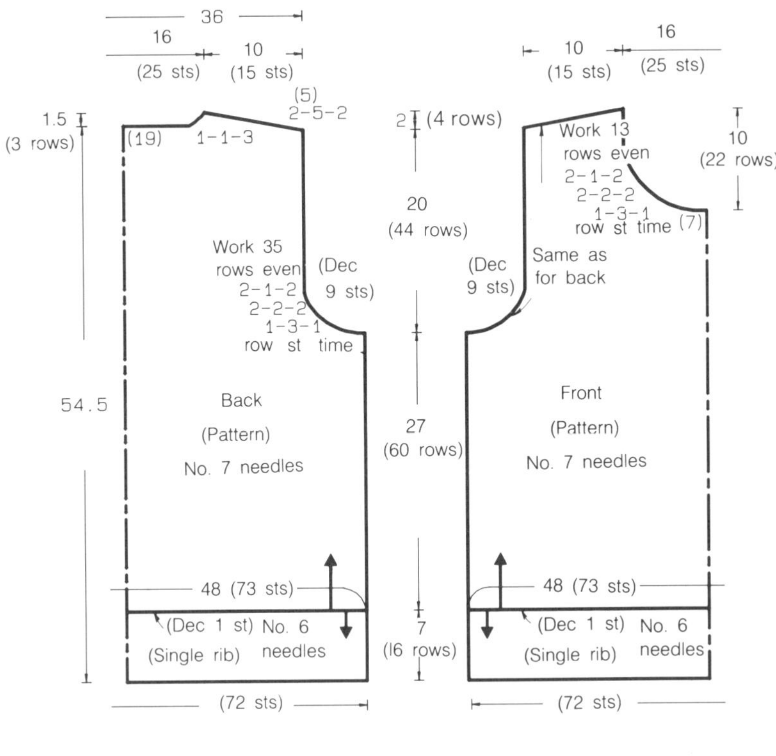

Pattern chart

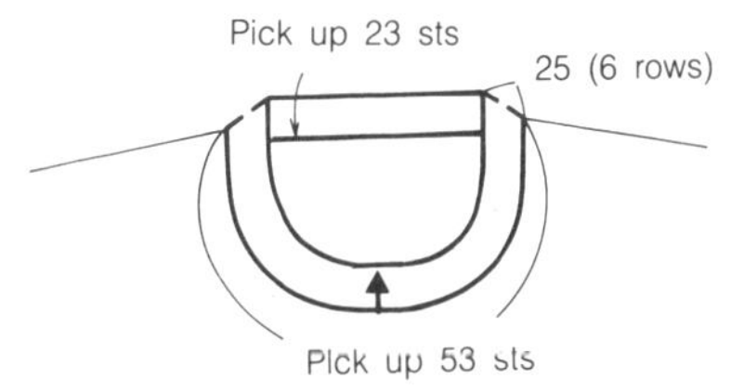
Neckband (single rib) No. 6 needles

27
Good Selections
Scallops in three tones of amber
make this a wondrous jacket.
★ Knit with "Bulky Yarn"
★ Directions on page 48.
Here's a sophisticated version of
the bulky look.
★ Knit with "Bulky Yarn"
★ Directions on page 49.
46

28

MATERIALS: "Bulky Yarn" 440g yarn variegated brown, light brown, and yellow, 240g grayish brown and 230g yellowish brown. 7 buttons 2.1cm in diameter.

NEEDLES: Knitting needles No. 9 and No. 8.

SIZES: Bust ... 112 cm. Width across back measurement ... 38cm. Length ... 63.5cm. Outside sleeve ... 54.5cm.

GAUGE: In 10cm square, 18 sts and 29.5 rows over pattern, 12 sts and 18 rows over garter st, and 16 sts and 20 rows over stockingette st.

DIRECTIONS: Work lower border, neck,

★ **Shown on page 46.**

center, and pocket band with 2 skeins of color A ; tweed yarn variegated brown, light brown and yellow, and other parts with 1 skein.

Front: Work sts separately to make pocket openings. Increase 1 st each with spiral st for pocket opening and work 46 rows, then work right and left together again. Decrease 1 st each for pocket opening on this row with 2 sts together.

Sleeve: Increase sts to shape sleeve lifting loop lying 1 st inside both ends of previous row.

Finishing: Darn inner pocket in pocket opening. Finish garter st with sl st using crochet hook on back side.

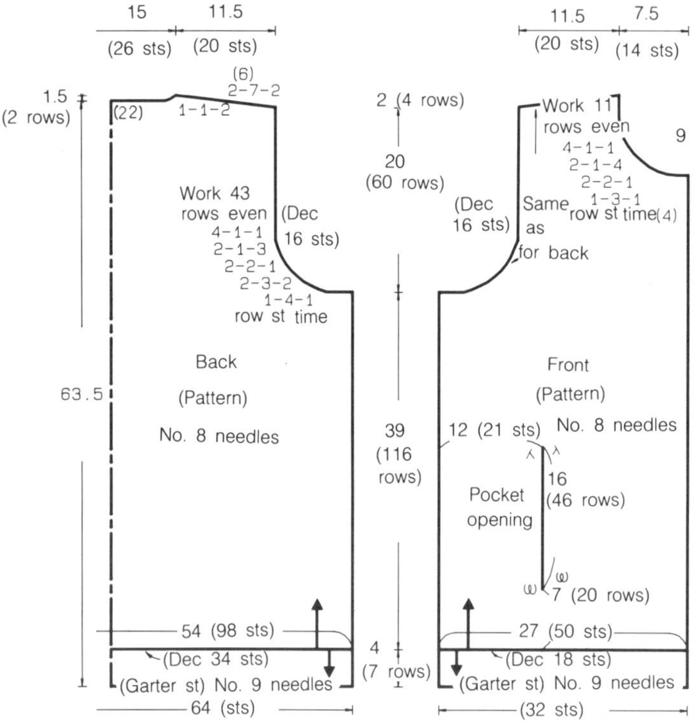

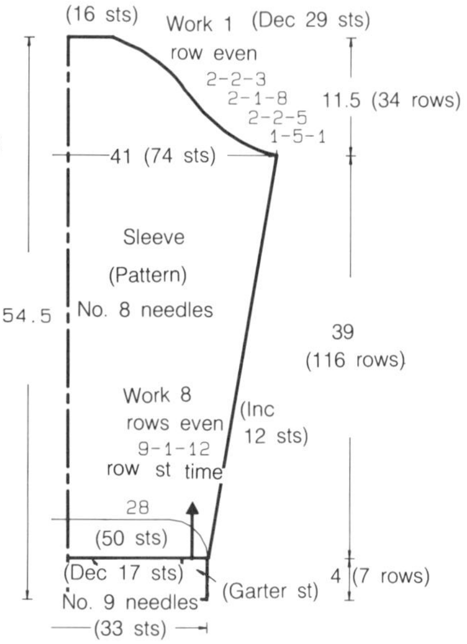

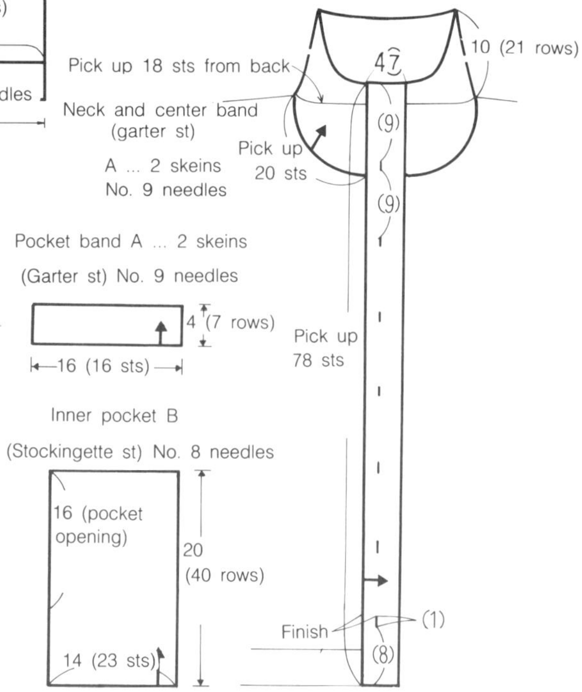

Pattern chart

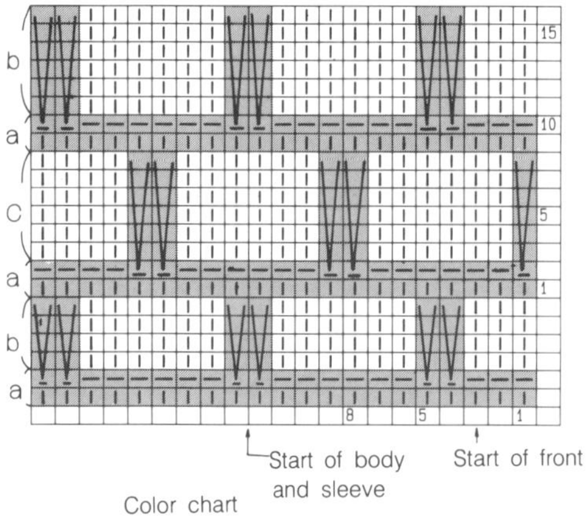

Color chart

A ... Yarn variegated brown, light brown, and yellow (tweed).
B ... Grayish brown
C ... Yellowish brown

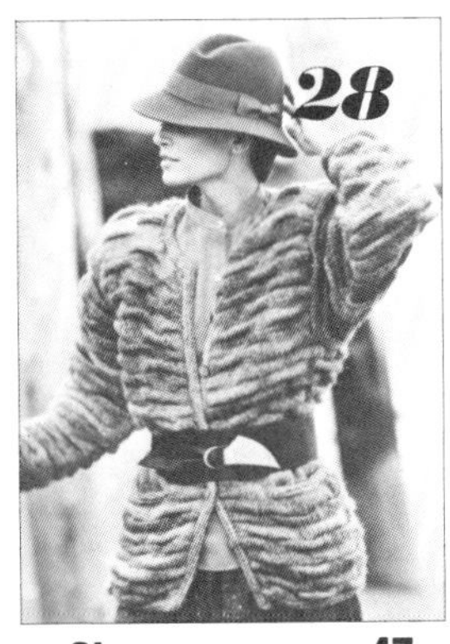

★ **Shown on page 47.**

MATERIALS: "Bulky Yarn" 880g ombre yarn of gray and dark green. 7 buttons 1.7cm in diameter.

NEEDLES: Knitting needles No. 7. Crochet hook No. 6.

SIZES: Bust ... 106cm. Width across back measurement ... 40cm. Length ... 62.5cm. Center of neck to wrist measurement ... 66.5cm.

GAUGE: 15 sts and 36 rows in 10cm square over pattern.

DIRECTIONS: Work pattern lifting needle loop lying 8 rows below on wrong side to shape wave on right side. Cast sts on needles, referring to the method on page 73. This is counted as the first row. Bind off 9 sts of underarm alternately at the beginning of the row. Work 1 row with another yarn for pocket opening. Work pocket band, picking up sts from sinker loops, and inner pocket, picking up sts from needle loops. Increase sts to shape sleeve, lifting the loop lying 1 st inside both ends of previous row. Join shoulder seam inside out with sl st using crochet hook. For edging, work sl st on row 1 and raised single crochet on back side on rows 3 to 5. The tops of single crochet run parallel. Set sleeves in body neatly with sl st. Work underarm in same manner.

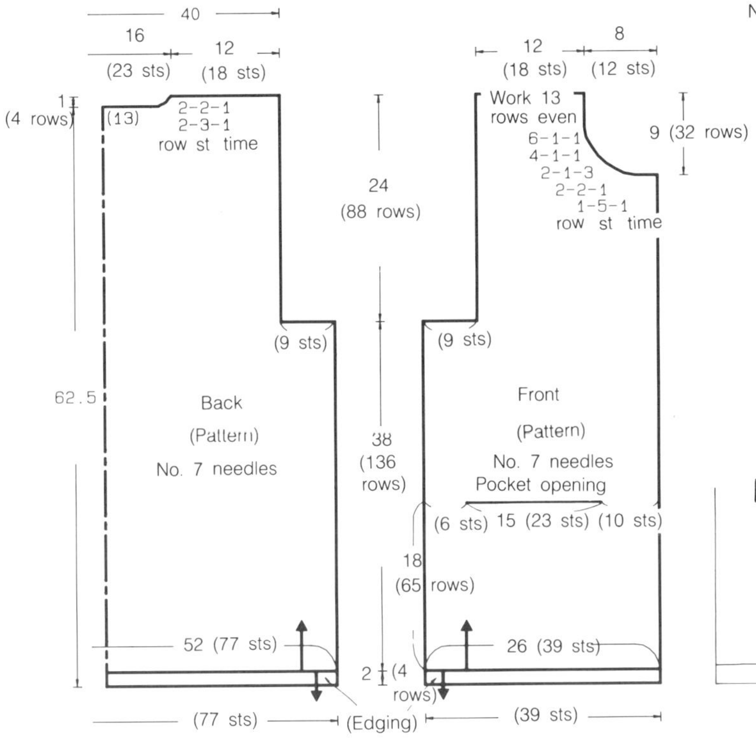

Neck and center band (edging) crochet hook No. 6

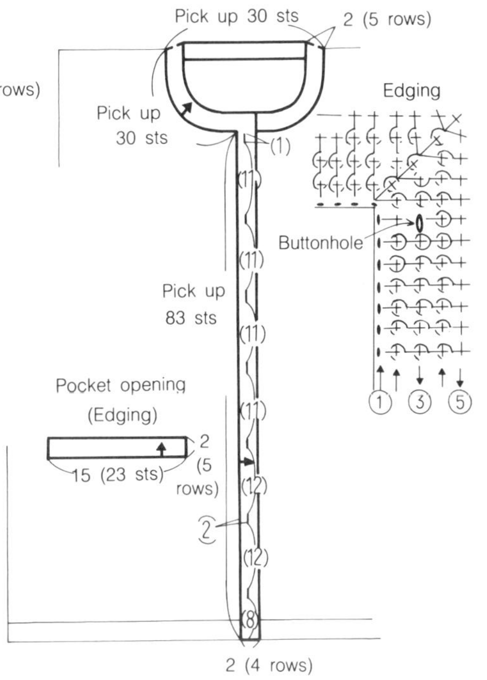

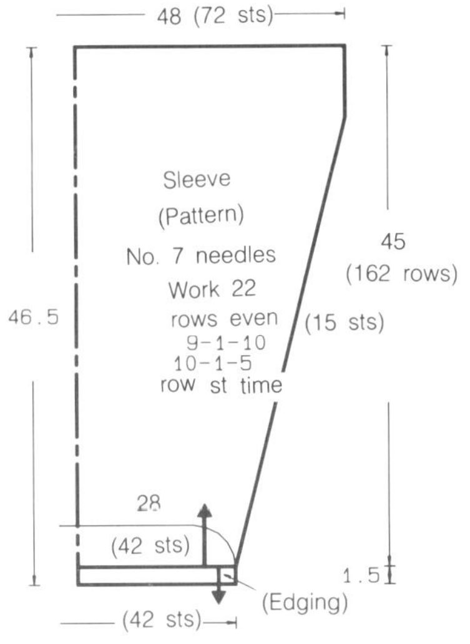

Inner pocket

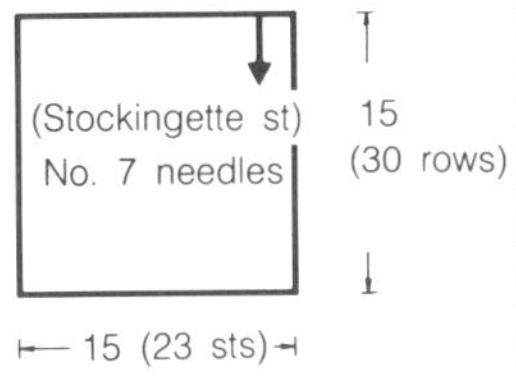

Pattern chart

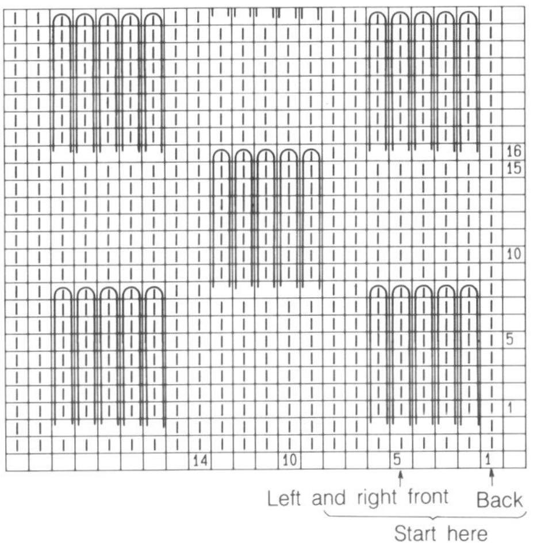

㉙ This pullover boasts graphi[c]
insets for outdoor fun.
★ Knit with "Bulky Yarn"
★ Directions on page 52.
㉚ Bold arrangements of color[ ]
individualist's triumph.
★ Knit with "Bulky Yarn"
★ Directions on page 53.

Favorite Knits

30

★ Shown on page 50.

MATERIALS: "Bulky Yarn" 380g charcoal gray, 120g bluish purple, 60g bluish green, and 50g each of grayish blue and mustard.
NEEDLES: Knitting needles No. 8 and No. 6.
SIZES: Bust ... 96cm. Length ... 55.5cm. Center of neck to wrist measurement ... 70cm.
GAUGE: 15 sts and 21 rows in 10cm square over color work. 15 sts and 24 rows in 10cm square over pattern.
DIRECTIONS: Make ch st with another yarn using crochet hook, and transfer sts from wrong side of ch to No. 8 needles. Take yarn not in use across the back of color work. Pull the yarn equally and cross 2 colors of yarn in same direction at 1 st before each changing color. Work rows even, up to neckline of body, place remaining center sts on holder; work right and left separately. Increase sts to shape sleeve, lifting the loop lying 1 st inside both ends of previous row. Unfasten the foundation ch, and pick up sts to work rib for body and wrist band toward opposite ends. Join shoulder seam inside out with sl st using crochet hook, then work neckband. Set sleeves in body joining sts and rows. Sew side and sleeve seam overcasting at every row. See page 74 concerning finishing of single rib.

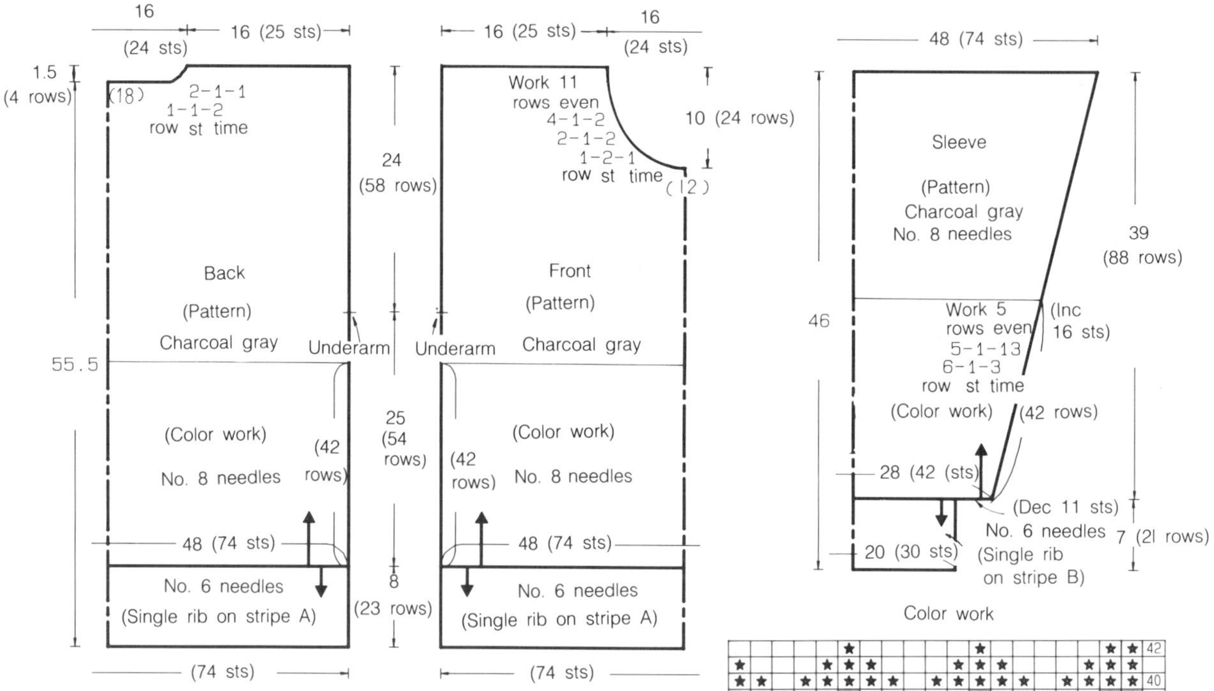

Pattern chart

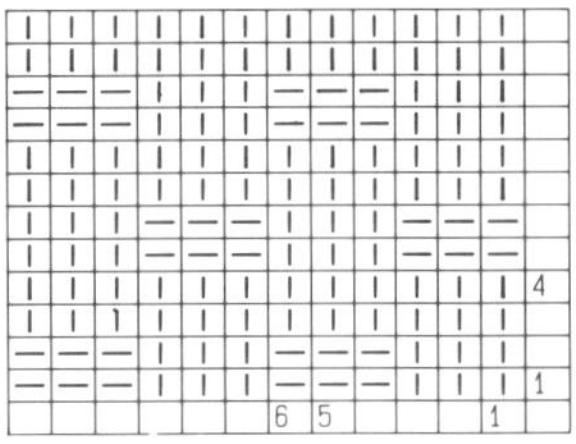

(Single rib on stripe A and B)

	A	B
Grayish blue	4 rows	4 rows
Charcoal gray	16	14
Mustard	2	2
Bluish purple	1	1
Total	23	21

Color work

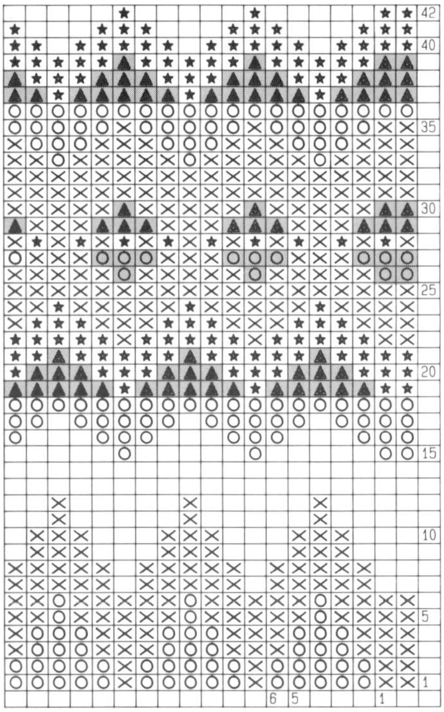

Neckband (single rib) No. 6 needles

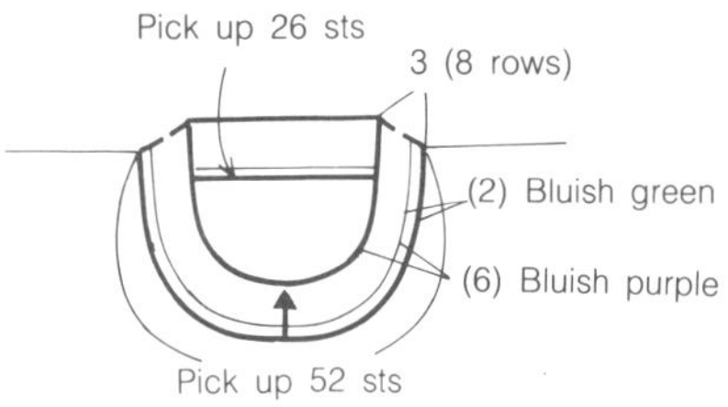

Color chart

- ☆ ...Mustard
- ▲ ...Grayish blue
- □ ...Charcoal gray
- ⊠ ...Bluish purple
- ○ ...Bluish green

▒ = Reversed stockingette st

★ **Shown on page 51.**

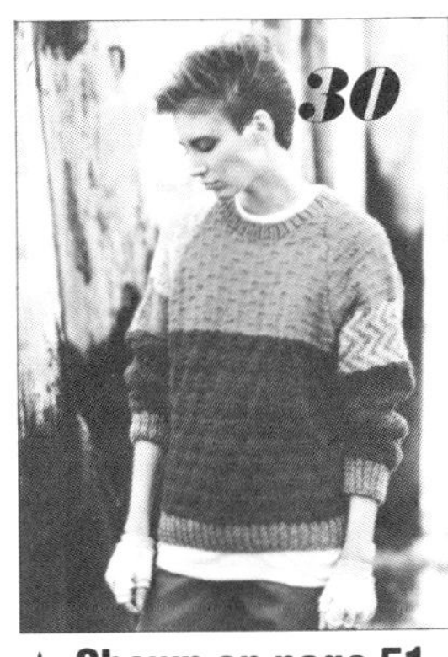

MATERIALS: "Bulky Yarn" 330g green, 140g purplish red, 130g gray, and 60g mustard.

NEEDLES: Knitting needles No. 9 and No. 8.

SIZES: Bust ... 98cm. Length ... 56.5cm. Center of neck to wrist measurement ... 73cm.

GAUGE: 15 sts and 20 rows in 10cm square over pattern A and B and over color work.

DIRECTIONS: Make ch sts with another yarn using crochet hook, and transfer sts from wrong side of ch to No. 9 needle to start body and sleeves. Work pattern A on body and sleeves with green, pattern B on body and left sleeve with purplish red, and pattern B on right sleeve with mustard. Note that color work is also different in color on right and left sleeves. Work 59 rows even up to underarm of body, and bind off 4 sts at the beginning of rows alternately to shape armholes. Increase sts to shape sleeve, lifting the loop lying 1 st inside both ends of previous row. Unfasten the foundation ch, and pick up sts to work rib of body and wrist toward opposite ends. Join raglan armholes with sl st using crochet hook, and work neckband. Pick up 72 sts, and work 6 rows circularly. See page 74 on finishing single rib.

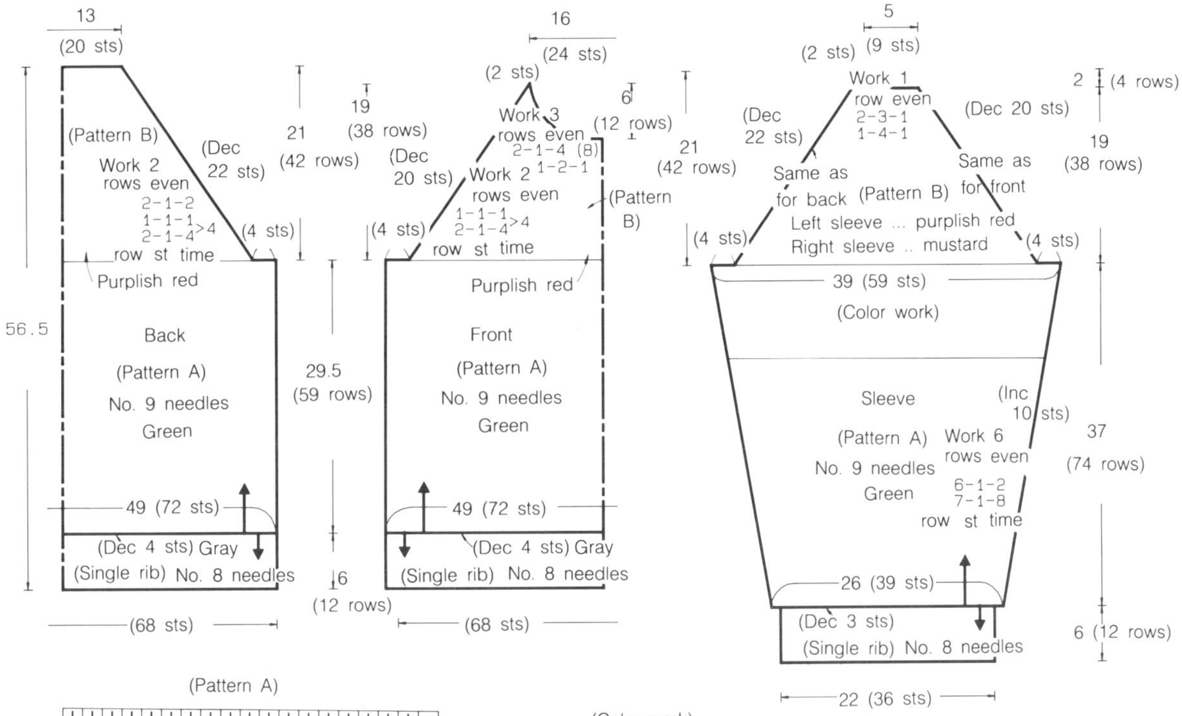

(Pattern A)

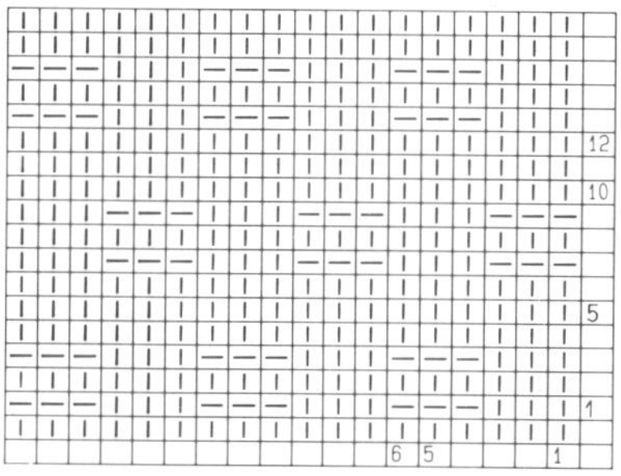

(Color work)

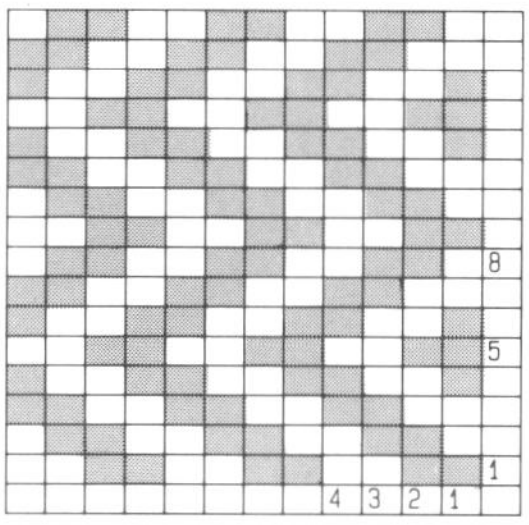

	Left sleeve	Right sleeve
(shaded) =	Mustard	Purplish red
(blank) =	Gray	Gray

(Pattern B)

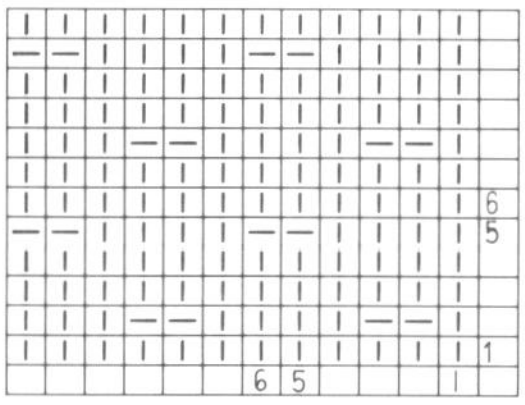

Neckband (single rib) gray No. 8 needles

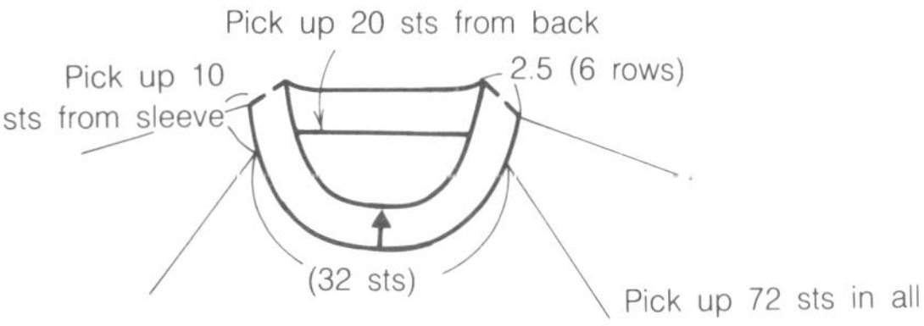

31

㉛ These dark-toned geometrics are positively wonderful.
★ Knit with "Bulky Yarn"
★ Directions on page 56.
㉜ Two colors make a beautiful contrast in pattern.
★ Knit with "Bulky Yarn"
★ Directions on page 57.

★ Shown on page 54.

MATERIALS: "Bulky Yarn" 180g charcoal gray, 140g each of gray, dark brown, and grayish brown, and 40g each of reddish purple and green.

NEEDLES: Knitting needles No. 7 and No. 6.

SIZES: Bust ... 100cm. Length ... 54.5 cm. Center of neck to wrist measurement ... 69cm.

GAUGE: 19 sts and 22 rows in 10cm square over color work.

DIRECTIONS: Make ch sts with another yarn using crochet hook, and transfer sts from wrong side of ch to No. 7 needle to start body and sleeves. Take yarn not in use across the back of color work. Pull the yarn equally and cross 2 colors in the same direction at 1 st before each change of color, referring to the diagram on page 74. Work rows even up to neckline, marking the points on underarm of body. Place remaining center sts of neckline on holder, and decrease right and left sts separately. Increase sts to shape sleeve, lifting the loop lying 1 st inside both ends of previous row. Unfasten the foundation ch and pick up sts to work rib of body and wrist band toward opposite ends. Bind off sts on the last row of sleeve cap, and set sleeves in body neatly with sl st using crochet hook.

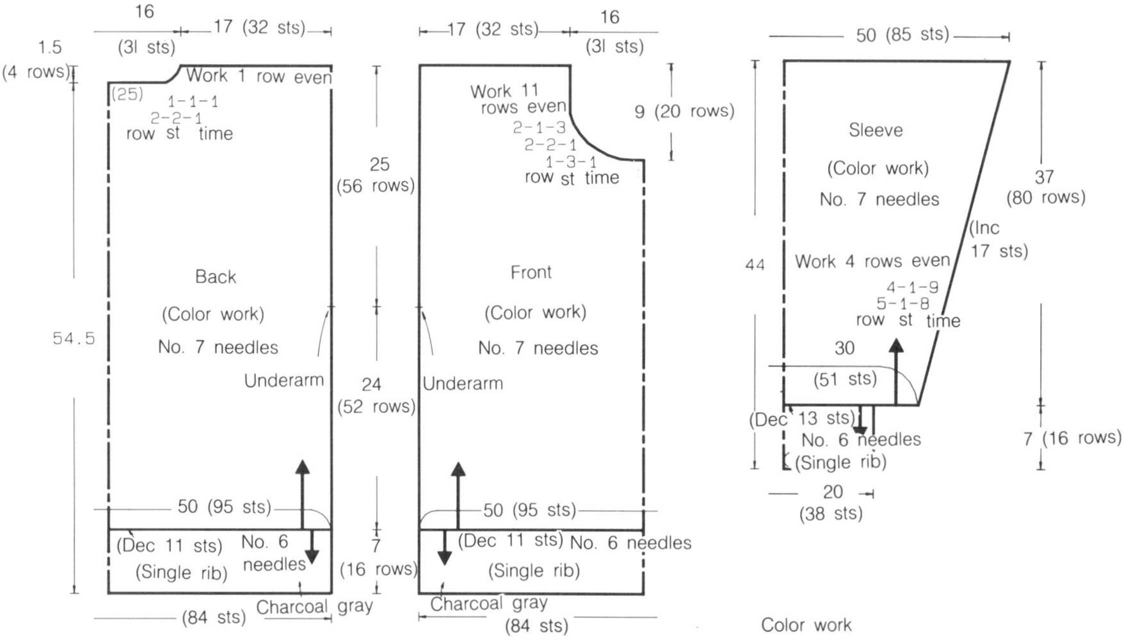

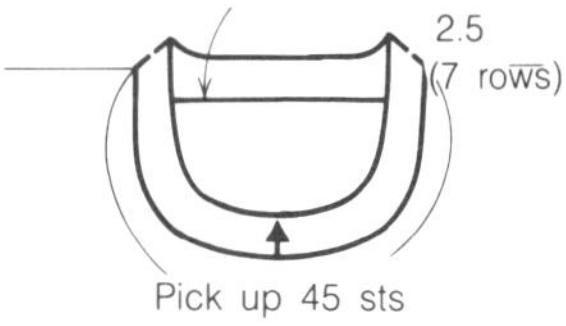

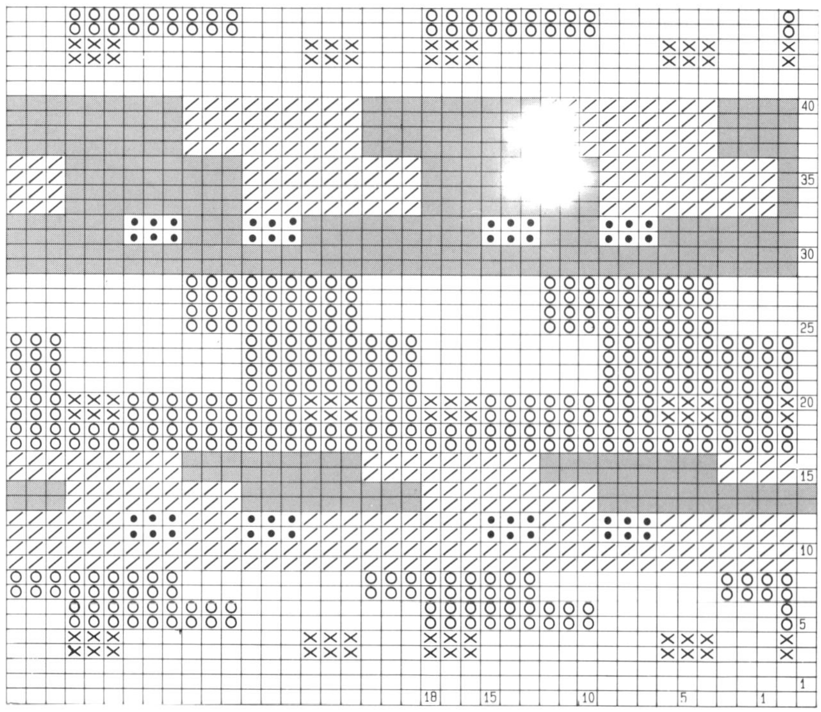

★ **Shown on page 55.**

MATERIALS: "Bulky Yarn" 380g grayish brown and 120g light brown.

NEEDLES: Knitting needles No. 8 and No. 7.

SIZES: Bust ... 96cm. Width across back measurement ... 35cm. Length ...56cm. Outside sleeve ... 54cm.

GAUGE: 14 sts and 18 rows in 10cm square over color work and stockingette st.

DIRECTIONS: Make ch sts with another yarn using crochet hook, and transfer sts from wrong side of ch to No. 8 needle. Purl sts at gray blocks in chart of color work so these sts make an uneven effect on pattern. Work 61 rows, referring to chart of color work, and continue to stockingette sts with grayish brown. In decreasing over 2 sts to shape armholes, bind off sts alternately at the beginning of row. Leave sts and turn to shape shoulder slope, referring to the diagram on page 74. Increase sts to shape sleeve, lifting the loop lying 1 st inside both ends of previous row. Unfasten the foundation ch and pick up sts to work rib toward opposite ends for lower border and wrist band. Join shoulder seam inside out with sl st using crochet hook, and work neckband. Pin sleeves in body neatly inside out and join with sl st.

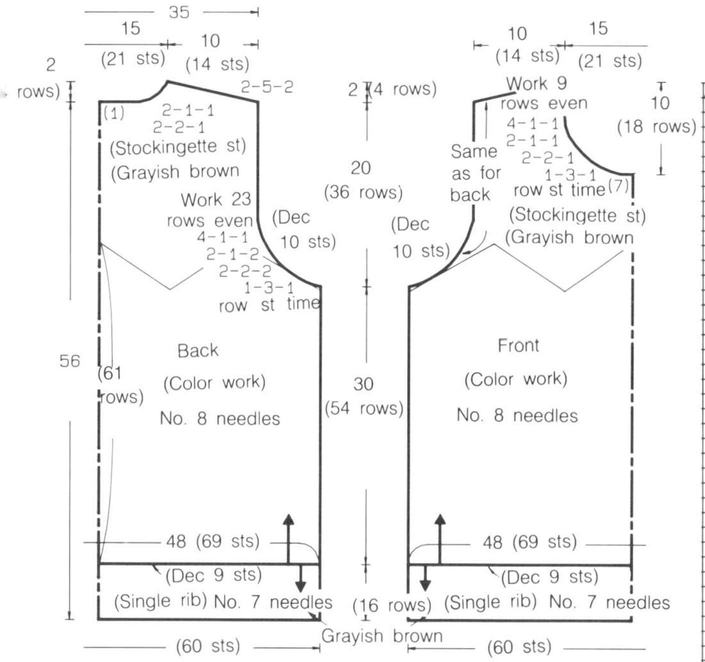

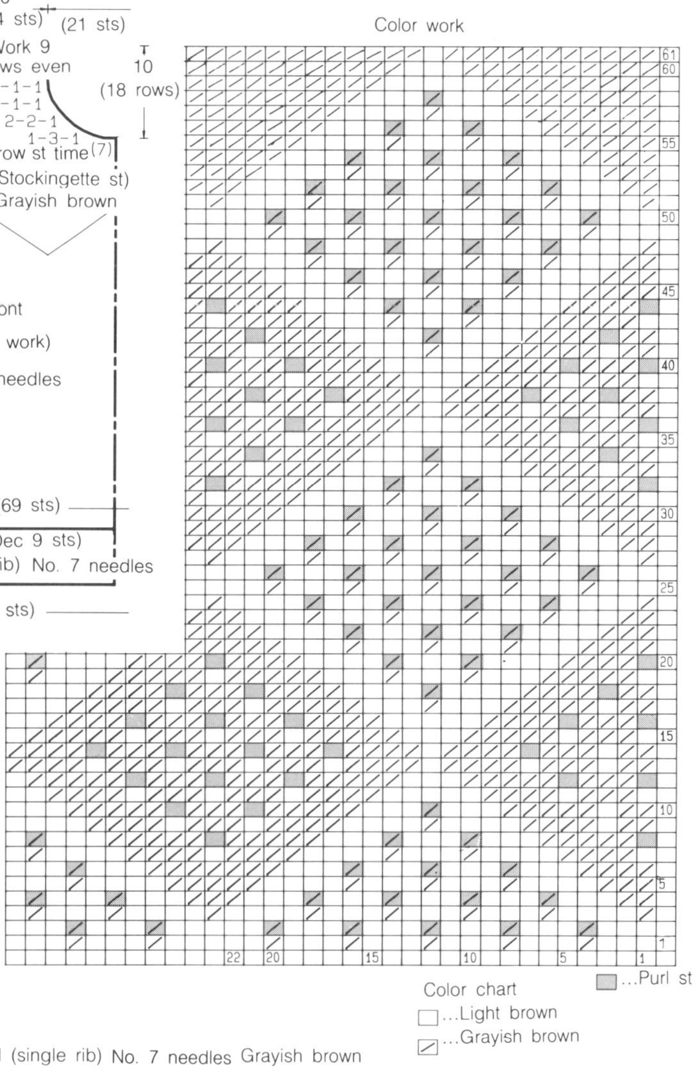

Back

Back (Color work) No. 8 needles

- 35
- 15 (21 sts)
- 10 (14 sts)
- 2 (4 rows)
- 2-5-2
- (1)
- 2-1-1
- 2-2-1
- (Stockingette st)
- (Grayish brown)
- Work 23 rows even
- 4-1-1
- 2-1-2
- 2-2-2
- 1-3-1 row st time
- (Dec 10 sts)
- 56 (61 rows)
- 48 (69 sts)
- (Dec 9 sts)
- (Single rib) No. 7 needles
- (60 sts)
- Grayish brown

Front

Front (Color work) No. 8 needles

- 10 (14 sts)
- 15 (21 sts)
- Work 9 rows even
- 4-1-1
- 2-1-1
- 2-2-1
- 1-3-1 row st time (7)
- 10 (18 rows)
- Same as for back
- (Stockingette st) (Grayish brown)
- 2 (4 rows)
- 20 (36 rows)
- (Dec 10 sts)
- 30 (54 rows)
- 48 (69 sts)
- (Dec 9 sts)
- (Single rib) No. 7 needles
- (60 sts)

Sleeve

Sleeve (Stockingette st) No. 8 needles Grayish brown

- (8 sts)
- Work 1 row even
- (Dec 21 sts)
- 2-3-1
- 2-2-2
- 2-1-5
- 2-2-3
- 1-3-1
- 13 (24 rows)
- 36 (50 sts)
- 54
- 35 (64 rows)
- Work 8 rows even
- 8-1-7 row st time
- (Inc 7 sts)
- 26
- (36 sts)
- (Dec 8 sts)
- No. 7 needles
- 6 (16 rows)
- (Single rib) Dark brown
- 40 (28 sts)

Color work

Color chart
- ☐ ...Light brown
- ⁄ ...Grayish brown
- ▧ ...Purl st

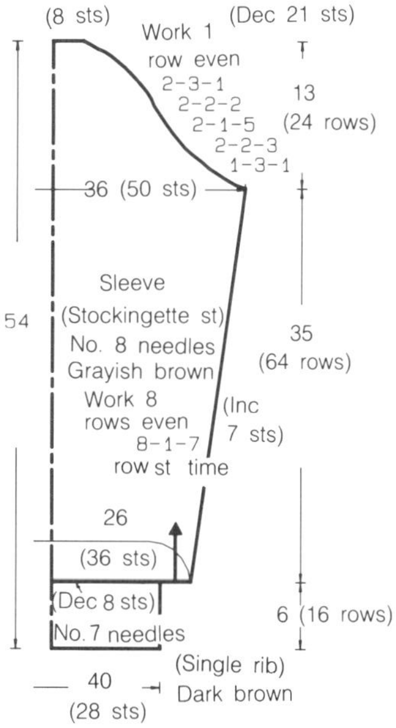

Neckband (single rib) No. 7 needles Grayish brown

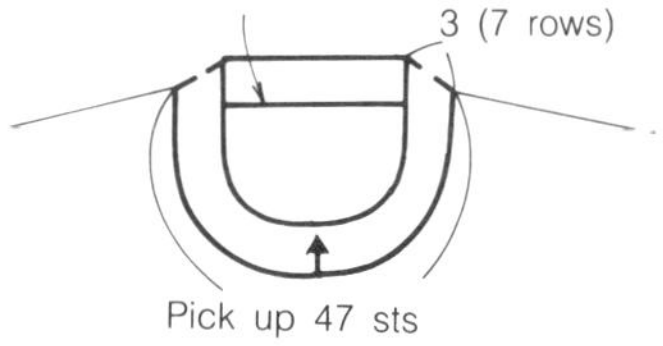

- Pick up 25 sts
- 3 (7 rows)
- Pick up 47 sts

㉝ Mohair stripes–a dreamy way to
stay warm and look lovely.
★ **Knit with "Bulky Yarn"**
★ **Directions on page 72.**

MATERIALS: "Sport Yarn" 270g ombre yarn with blue, reddish purple, bluish green, orange, etc.

NEEDLES: Knitting needles No. 7 and No. 4–5.

SIZES: Bust ... 100cm. Length ... 55cm. Center of neck to wrist measurement ... 70cm.

GAUGE: 12 sts and 38 rows 10 cm square over pattern.

DIRECTIONS: Make ch sts with another yarn using crochet hook, and transfer sts from wrong side of ch to No. 7 needle. One repeat of pattern consists of 3 sts and 4 rows working 2 garter sts and 1 raised st of 3 rows. The row picked up from ch is counted as row 1. On row 2, repeat to knit 2 sts (to become loop of garter st on right side) and to cast on 1 st. Continue rows 3 and 4 in same manner. On row 5, knit all sts on right side. Knit remaining sts on right side and crossing 3 yarns on back side. Work rows even up to neckline marking the point on underarm of body. Unfasten the foundation ch and pick up sts from 1 st row to work rib of body and wrist band toward opposite ends. (See page 73.) Join shoulder seam with sl st using crochet hook, and work neckband circularly, referring to the diagram below. Set sleeves in body neatly with sl st, and sew side and sleeve seam with overcasting st.

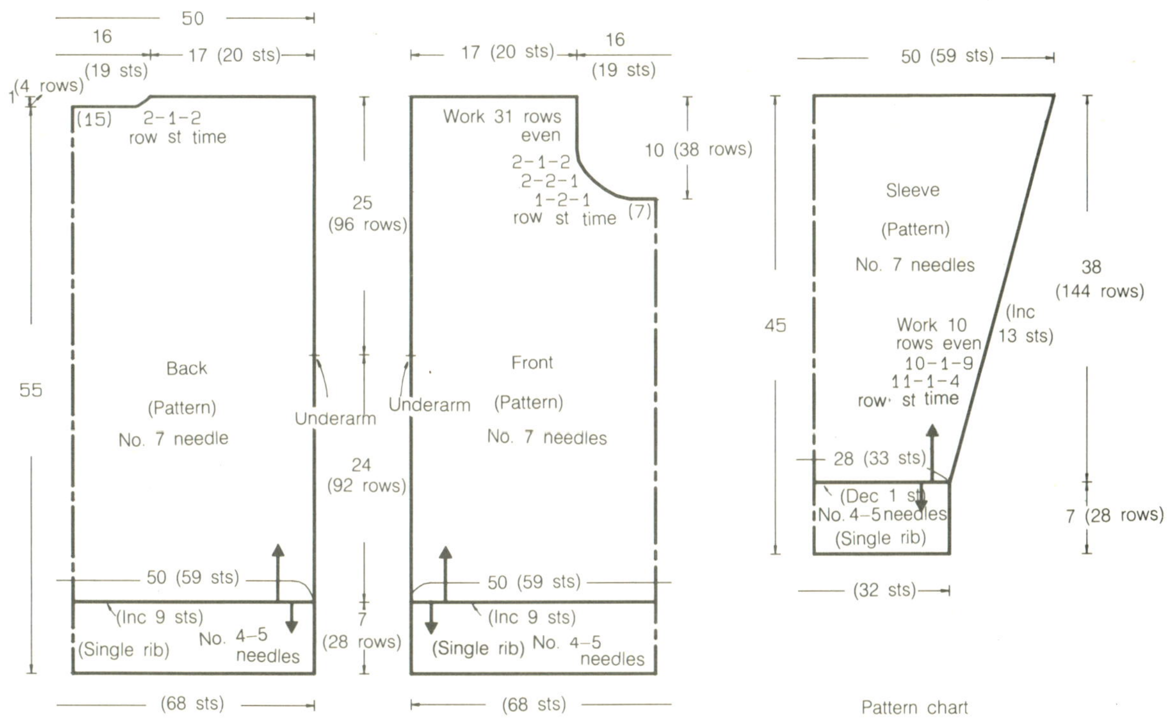

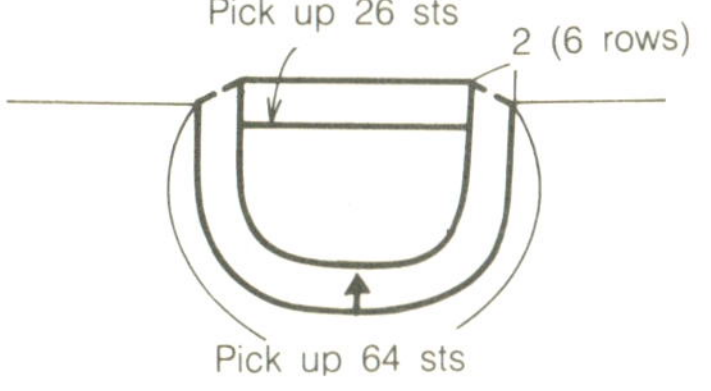
Neckband (single rib) No. 4–5 needles

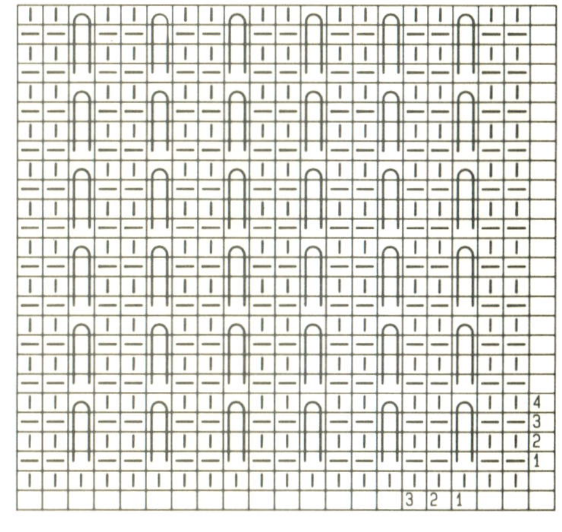
Pattern chart

★ **Shown on page 3.**

MATERIALS: "Sport Yarn" 250g ombre yarn with off-white, yellow, orange, purple, blue, etc.
NEEDLES: Knitting needles No. 7 and No. 6.
SIZES: Bust ... 96cm. Length ... 53.5cm. Center of neck to wrist measurement ... 70cm.
GAUGE: 21 sts and 22 rows in 10cm square over pattern A and B. 15 sts and 22 rows in 10cm square over stockingette st.
DIRECTIONS: Make ch sts with another yarn using crochet hook, and transfer sts from wrong side of ch to start body and sleeves. Change patterns from A to B on body to make V shape symmetrically. Work rows even up to neckline, marking the points on underarm of body. Work pattern A on the center of sleeves and stockingette st on both sides. Increase sts to shape sleeves, lifting the loop lying 1 st inside both ends of previous row. Unfasten the foundation ch and pick up sts from the first row to work rib of body and wrist band toward opposite ends. Decrease required sts with 2 sts together equally on the first row of rib. Join shoulder seam with sl st using crochet hook, and pick up 92 sts from neckline of body to work rib circularly. Set sleeves inside out in determined position of body with sl st. Sew side and sleeve seam overcasting st every row.

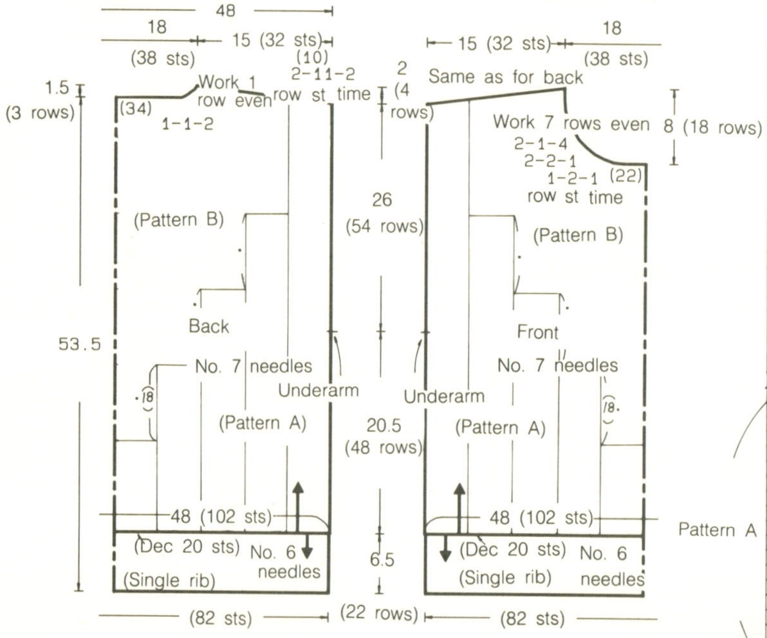

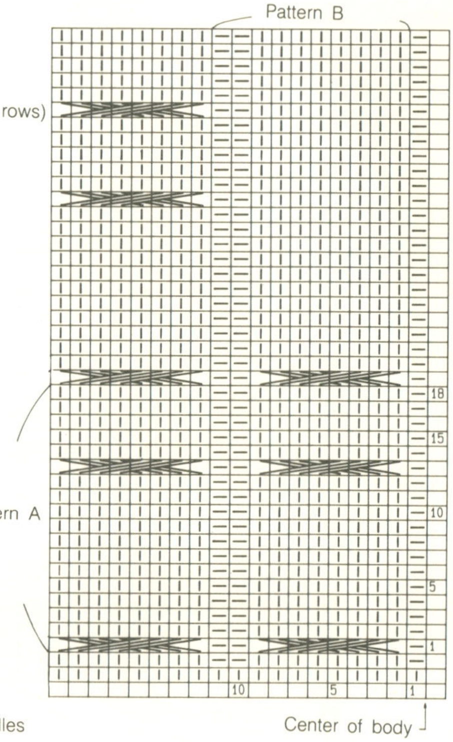

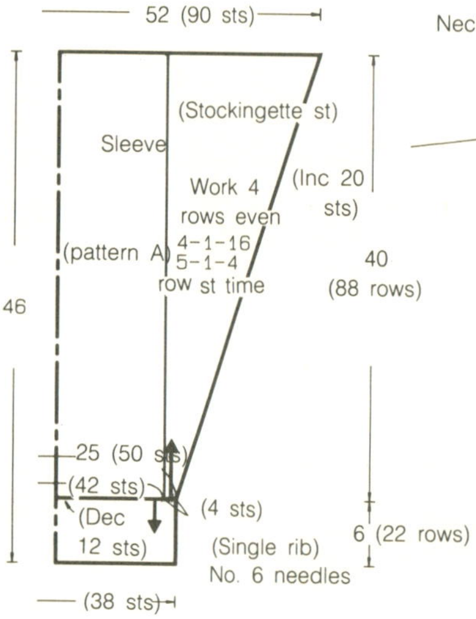

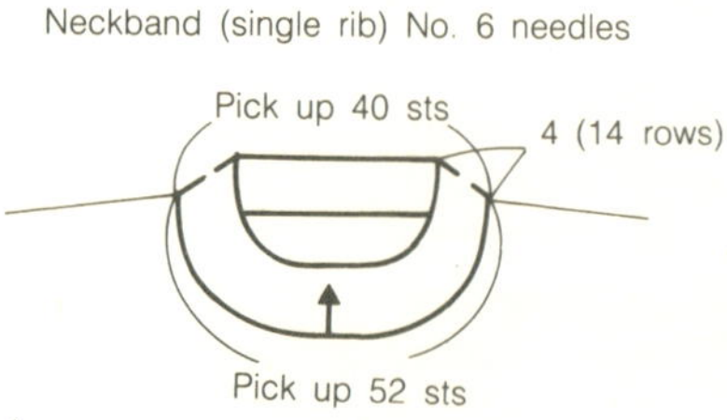

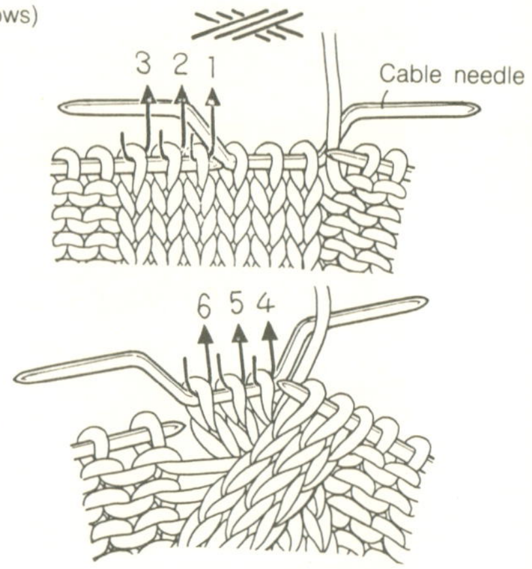

MATERIALS: "Bulky Yarn" 400g ombre yarn with cherry pink, bluish purple, reddish purple, green, yellowish green, etc. (701).
NEEDLES: Knitting needles No. 7 and No. 4–5.
SIZES: Bust ... 96cm. Width across back measurement ... 38cm. Length 55cm. Outside sleeve ... 53cm.
GAUGE: 18 sts and 24 rows in 10cm square over pattern.
DIRECTIONS: Make ch sts with another yarn using crochet hook, transfer sts from wrong side of ch to No. 7 needle, and start body and sleeve. Work spiral st at the border between knit st, and purl st of triangular pattern and work 3 sts together with center st front at the center of knit st. Work rows even up to underarm; then decrease sts to shape armholes. In decreasing over 2 sts, bind off sts alternately at the beginning of rows. Place remaining center sts on holder, and work right and left separately, decreasing sts at the beginning of rows to shape neckline. Increase sts to shape sleeve, lifting the loop lying 1 st inside both ends of previous row. Unfasten the foundation ch, and pick up sts to work rib of body and wrist band toward opposite ends. Join shoulder seam inside out with sl st using crochet hook. Pick up 84 sts from neckline, and work 6 rows circularly. Pin sleeves neatly in body inside out and join with sl st.

★ **Shown on page 4.**

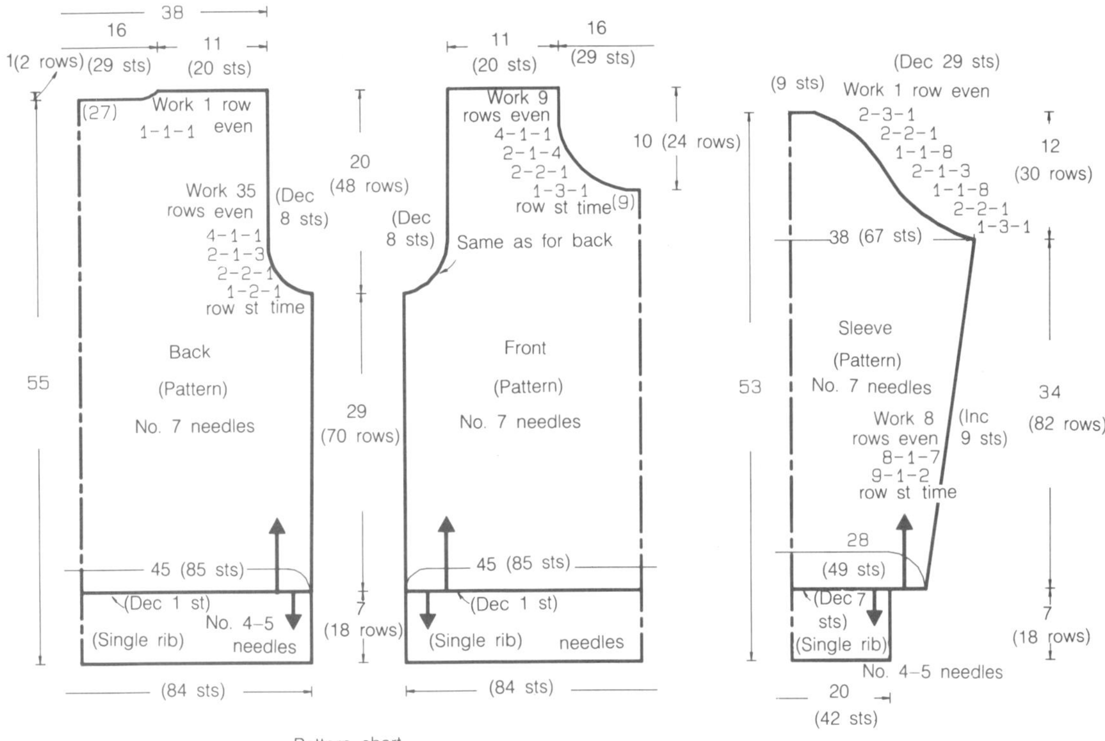

Pattern chart

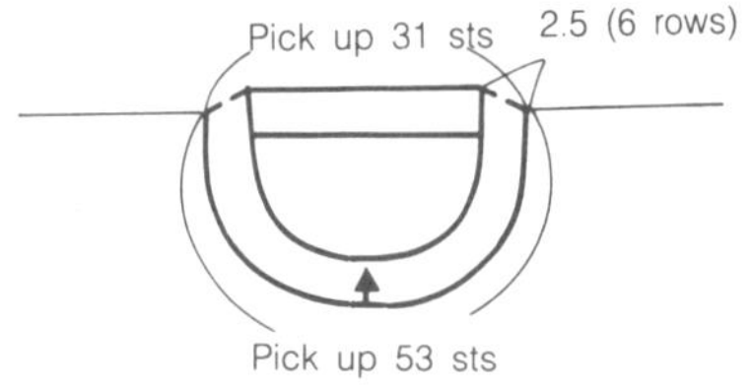

Neckband (single rib) No. 4–5 needles

MATERIALS: "Sport Yarn" 400g gray.
NEEDLES: Knitting needles No. 7 and No. 4–5.
SIZES: Bust ... 96cm. Width across back measurement ... 36cm. Length ... 57cm. Outsides sleeve ... 53cm.
GAUGE: 18 sts and 23 rows in 10cm square over pattern.
DIRECTIONS: Make ch sts with another yarn using crochet hook, and transfer sts from wrong side of ch to No. 7 needle. Work 68 rows even up to underarm; then decrease sts to shape armholes. In decreasing over 2 sts, bind off sts at the beginning of row alternately. Place remaining center sts on holder, and work right and left separately, decreasing sts at the beginning of rows to shape neckline. Increase sts to shape sleeve, lifting the loop lying 1 st inside both ends of previous row. Make body and sleeves; then unfasten the foundation ch and pick up sts to work single rib toward opposite end. Join shoulder seam inside out with sl st using crochet hook. Pick up 76 sts from neckline, and work 8 rows circularly. Pin sleeves neatly in body inside out and join with sl st. Iron out the work lightly to shape. See page 74 on finishing single rib.

★ **Shown on page 5.**

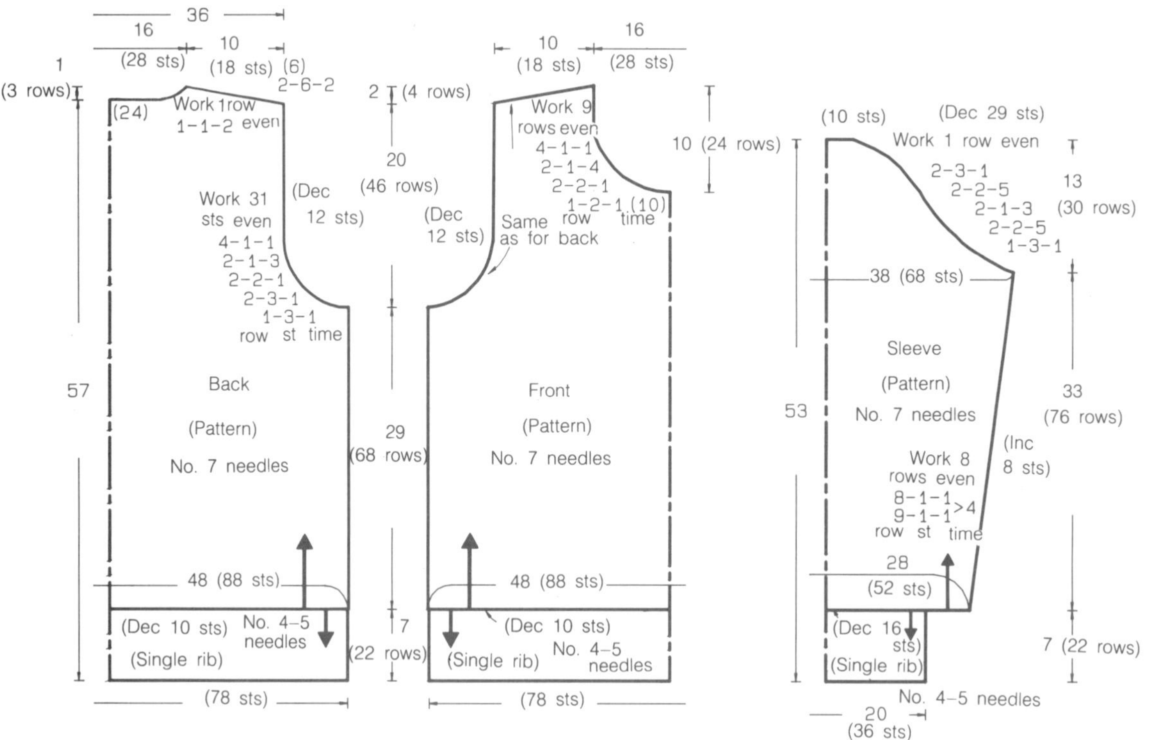

Pattern chart

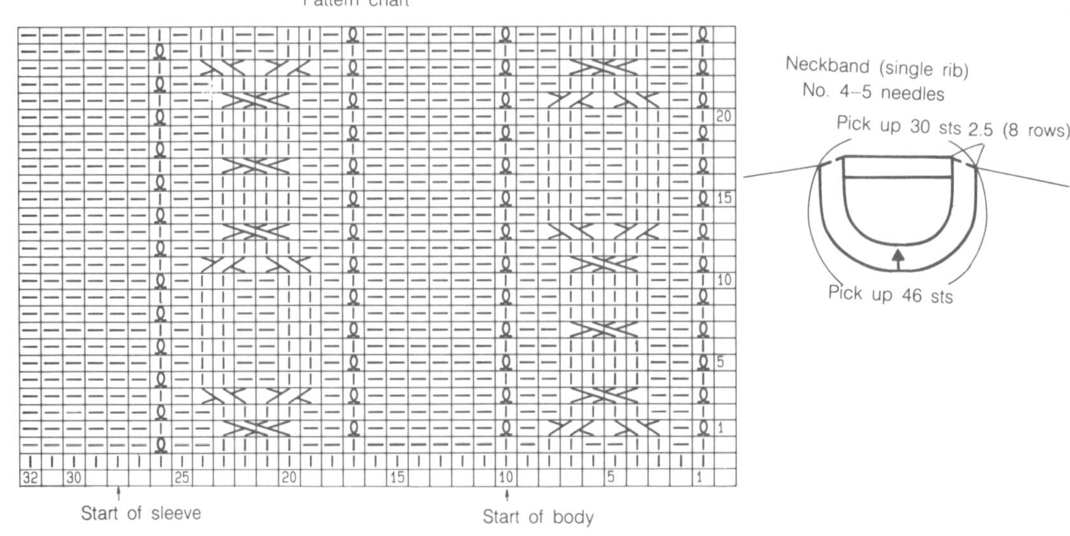

★ **Shown on page 6.**

MATERIALS: "Sport Yarn" 450g yarn variegated grayish pink, dull rose, bluish purple, red, blue, etc.
NEEDLES: Knitting needles No. 7 and No. 4–5.
SIZES: Bust ... 100cm. Length ... 55cm. Center of neck to wrist measurement ...70cm.
GAUGE: 17 sts and 20 rows in 10cm square over pattern.
DIRECTIONS: Make ch sts with another yarn using crochet hook and transfer sts from wrong side of ch to No. 7 needle. Note the starting sts of body and sleeves in pattern. Work rows even up to neckline, marking the points of underarm of body. Place remaining center sts on holder, and work right and left separately, decreasing sts at the beginning of row to shape neckline. Increase sts to shape sleeve, lifting the loop lying 1 st inside both ends of previous row. Make 76 rows of sleeve and bind off. Unfasten the foundation ch and pick up sts to work single rib of lower border and wrist band toward opposite ends. Join shoulder seam inside out with sl st using crochet hook. Pick up 92 sts from neckline, and work 6 rows circularly. Pin sleeves neatly in body and join with sl st. Sew side and sleeve seam with overcasting st.

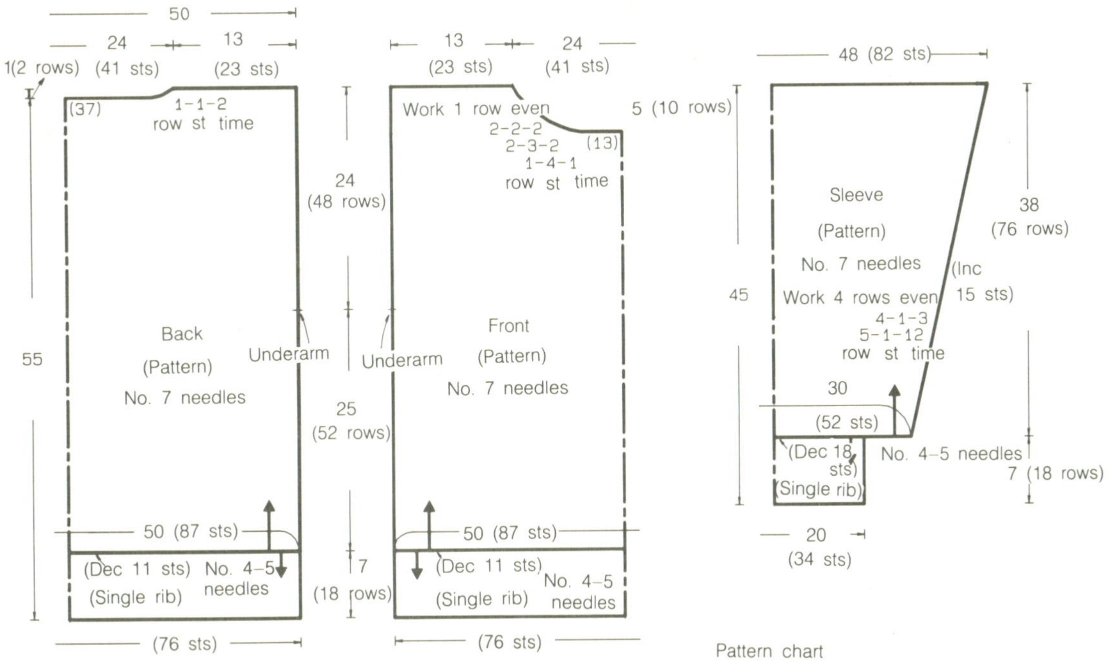

Back

- 50
- 24 (41 sts) 13 (23 sts)
- 1 (2 rows)
- (37)
- 1–1–2 row st time
- 55
- 24 (48 rows)
- Back (Pattern) No. 7 needles
- Underarm
- 50 (87 sts)
- (Dec 11 sts) (Single rib) No. 4–5 needles
- (76 sts)

Front

- 13 (23 sts) 24 (41 sts)
- Work 1 row even
- 2–2–2
- 2–3–2 (13)
- 1–4–1 row st time
- 5 (10 rows)
- 24 (48 rows)
- Underarm
- Front (Pattern) No. 7 needles
- 25 (52 rows)
- 50 (87 sts)
- (Dec 11 sts) (Single rib) No. 4–5 needles
- 7 (18 rows)
- (76 sts)

Sleeve

- 48 (82 sts)
- Sleeve (Pattern) No. 7 needles
- 45
- Work 4 rows even
- 4–1–3
- 5–1–12 row st time
- 38 (76 rows)
- (Inc 15 sts)
- 30 (52 sts)
- (Dec 18 sts) (Single rib)
- No. 4–5 needles
- 7 (18 rows)
- 20 (34 sts)

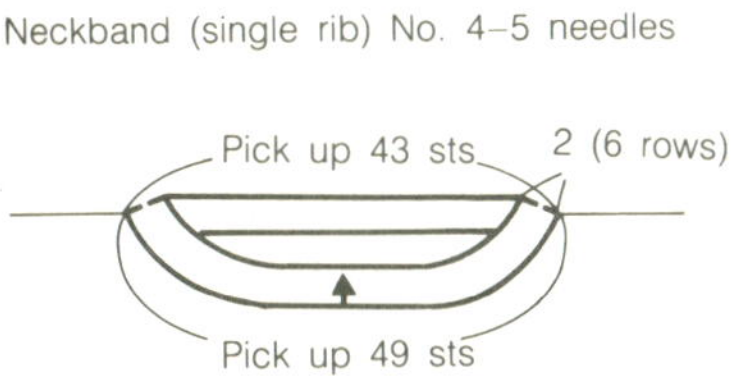

Neckband (single rib) No. 4–5 needles

- Pick up 43 sts
- 2 (6 rows)
- Pick up 49 sts

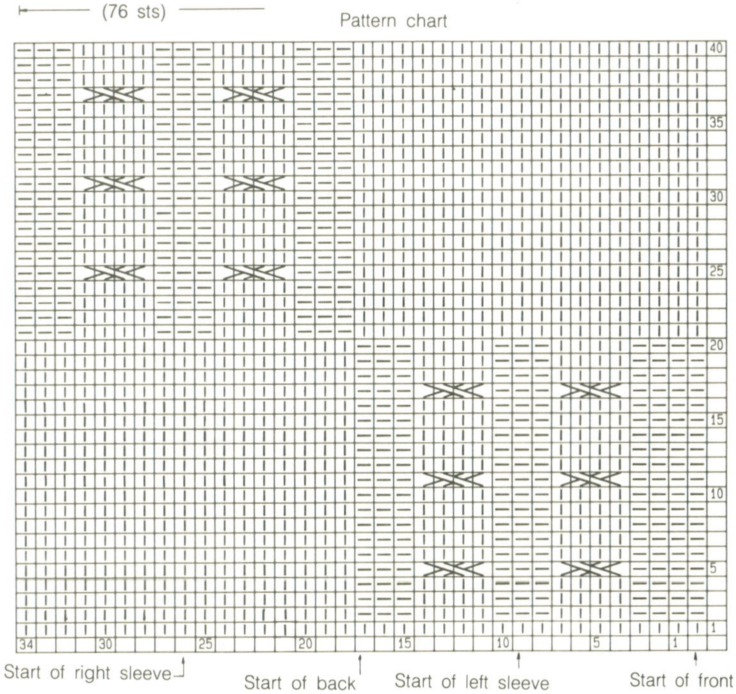

Pattern chart

Start of right sleeve Start of back Start of left sleeve Start of front

★ **Shown on page 7.**

MATERIALS: "Bulky Yarn" 400g pale gray.
NEEDLES: Knitting needles No. 7 and No. 4–5.
SIZES: Bust ... 96cm. Length ... 54.5cm. Center of neck to wrist ... 66cm.
GAUGE: 17 sts and 24 rows in 10cm square.
DIRECTIONS: Make ch sts with another yarn using crochet hook, and transfer sts from wrong side of ch to No. 7 needle. At the determined points of popcorn balls, repeat 1 knit st and 1 purl st in 1 st of previous row 2 times, then work 4 sts and 5 rows for each ball. Work rows even up to neckline, marking the points on underarm of body. Place remaining center sts on holder and work right and left separately, decreasing sts at the beginning of rows to shape neckline. Increase sts to shape sleeve, lifting the loop lying 1 st inside both ends of previous row. Make sleeve and place sts on holder. Unfasten the foundation ch, and pick up sts from sinker loop of the first row to work rib for body and wrist band toward opposite ends. Join shoulder seam with sl st using crochet hook, and work neckband. Set sleeves in body, grafting sts and rows with stockingette st as shown on page 73. Be sure to pick up 1 st inside from edge of body.

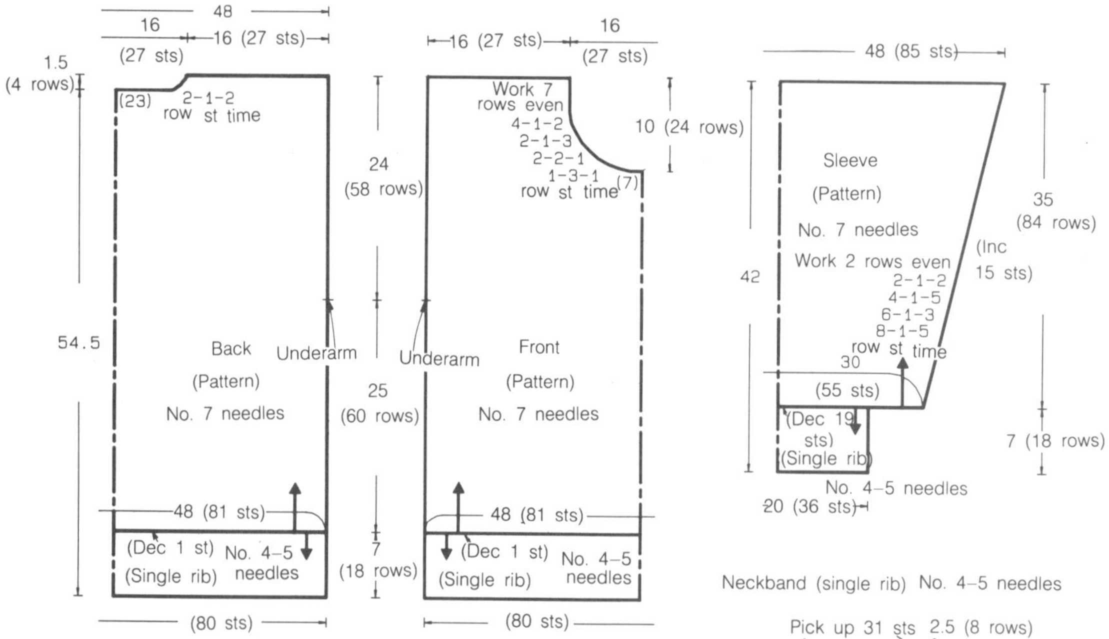

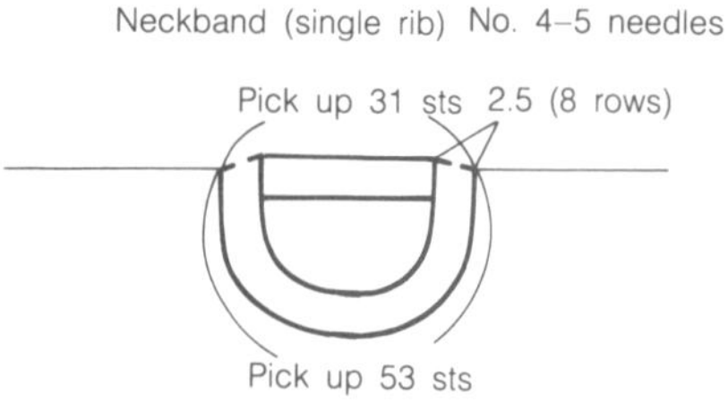

Schematic diagrams

Back (Pattern) No. 7 needles
- 16 (27 sts), 48, 16 (27 sts)
- 1.5 (4 rows)
- (23) 2-1-2 row st time
- 24 (58 rows)
- 54.5
- Underarm
- 25 (60 rows)
- 48 (81 sts) (Dec 1 st) No. 4–5 needles (Single rib)
- 7 (18 rows)
- (80 sts)

Front (Pattern) No. 7 needles
- 16 (27 sts), 16 (27 sts)
- Work 7 rows even
- 4-1-2
- 2-1-3
- 2-2-1
- 1-3-1 row st time (7)
- 10 (24 rows)
- Underarm
- 48 (81 sts) (Dec 1 st) No. 4–5 needles (Single rib)
- (80 sts)

Sleeve (Pattern) No. 7 needles
- 48 (85 sts)
- Work 2 rows even
- 2-1-2
- 4-1-5
- 6-1-3
- 8-1-5 row st time
- 35 (84 rows)
- (Inc 15 sts)
- 42
- 30 (55 sts)
- (Dec 19 sts) (Single rib)
- 7 (18 rows)
- 20 (36 sts)
- No. 4–5 needles

Neckband (single rib) No. 4–5 needles
- Pick up 31 sts 2.5 (8 rows)
- Pick up 53 sts

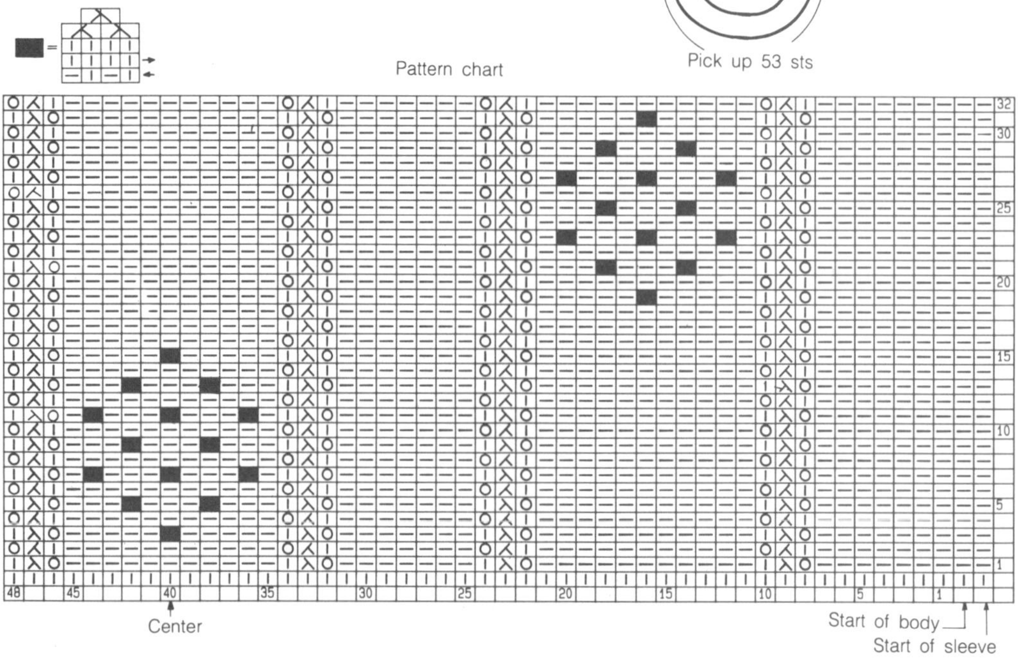

Pattern chart

Center

Start of body
Start of sleeve

★ **Shown on page 8.**

MATERIALS: "Bulky Yarn" 550g yarn variegated bluish purple, greenish blue, green, off-white, etc. in grayish olive. 6 buttons 1.5cm in diameter.

NEEDLES: Knitting needles No. 7.

SIZES: Bust ... 102cm. Width across back measurement ... 38cm. Length ... 53.5cm. Outside sleeve ... 50.5cm.

GAUGE: 15 sts and 23 rows in 10cm square over stockingette st and pattern.

DIRECTIONS: Make ch sts with another ch using crochet hook, and transfer sts from wrong loop of ch to No. 7 needle. At the determined points of popcorn ball, work 5 sts of knit 1, purl 1, knit 1, purl 1, and knit 1 in

1 st of previous row, and work 5 rows only, these 5 sts to make ball. Bind off over 2 sts alternately at the beginning of row to shape armhole. See diagram on page 74 on leaving sts on shoulder slope. Increase sts to shape sleeve, lifting the loop lying 1 st inside both ends of previous row. Join shoulder seam with sl st using crochet hook, and work neckband. Pick up 87 sts from neckband, body, and lower border to work center band. Make buttonholes on center band of right front shown below. Sew side and sleeve seam with overcasting st, and set sleeve in body neatly with sl st.

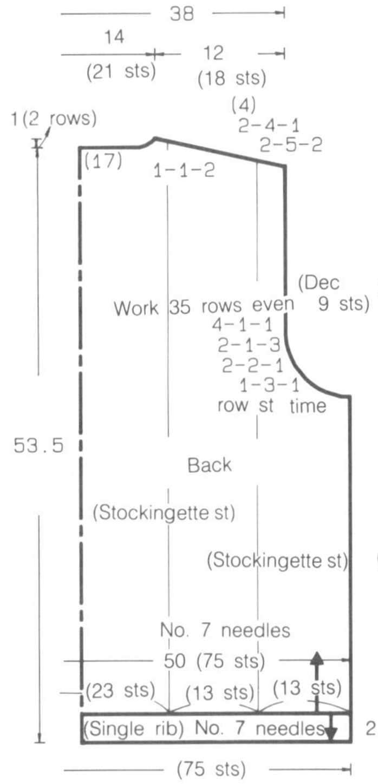

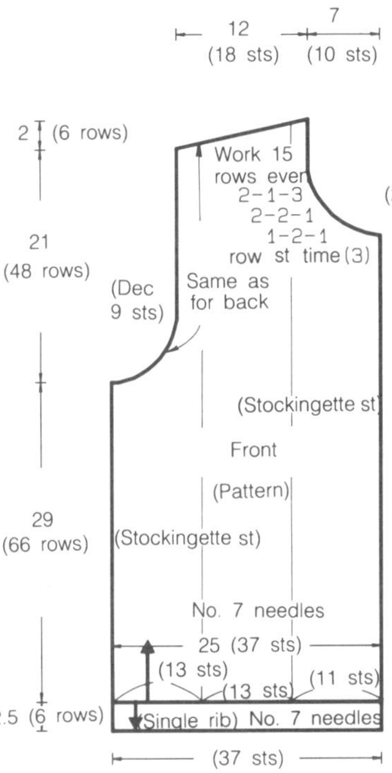

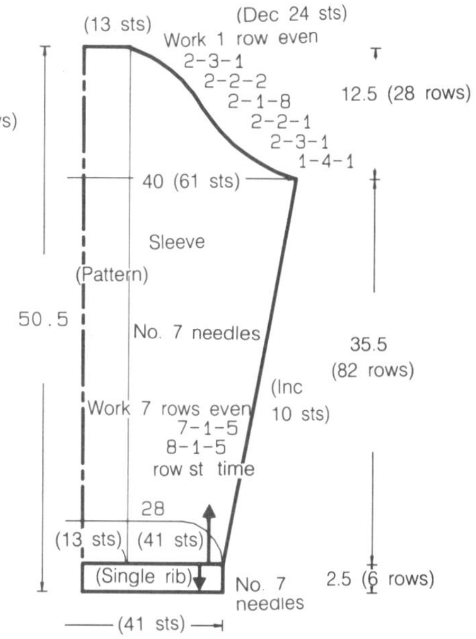

Pattern chart

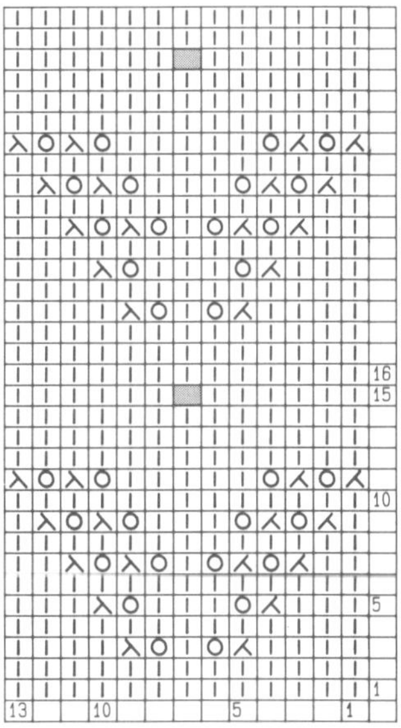

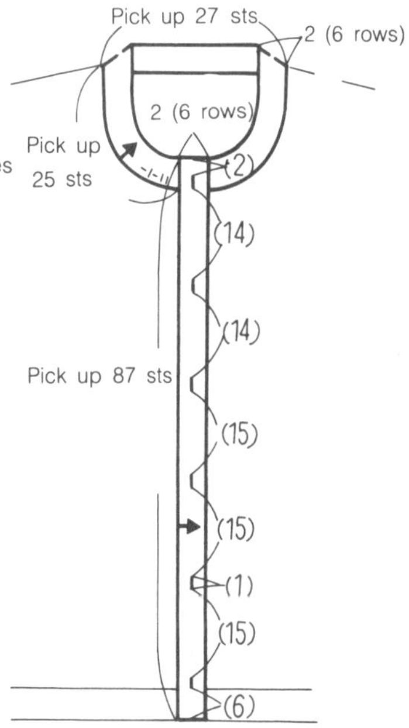

Buttonhole

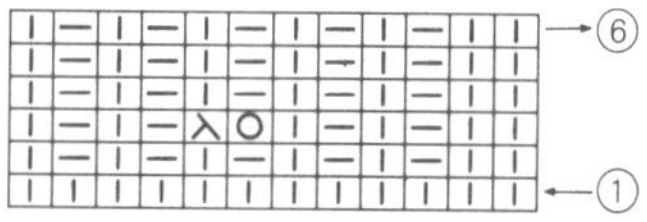

Bottom edge

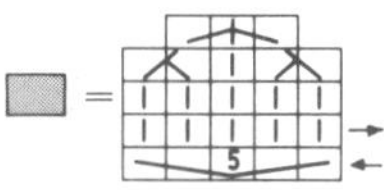

Neck and center band (single rib) No. 7 needles

Sleeve (Pattern) No. 7 needles

Back (Stockingette st) (Stockingette st) No. 7 needles

Front (Stockingette st) (Pattern) (Stockingette st) No. 7 needles

★ **Shown on page 9.**

MATERIALS: "Bulky Yarn" 650g yarn variegated light brown, rose, white, blue, reddish purple, etc. 7 buttons 1.7cm in diameter.

NEEDLES: Knitting needles No. 10½ and No. 8.

SIZES: Bust ... 105cm. Width across back measurement ... 38cm. Length ... 57cm. Outside sleeve ... 54cm.

GAUGE: 11.5 sts and 18 rows in 10cm square over stockingette st. 15 sts and 18 rows in 10cm square over pattern.

DIRECTIONS: Make ch sts with another yarn using crochet hook, and transfer sts from wrong side of ch to No. 10½ needle. Work reversed stockingette st on back body. Work pattern at determined position on front body. In decreasing over 2 sts to shape armhole, bind off sts at the beginning of row alternately. Increase sts to shape sleeve, lifting the loop lying 1 st inside both ends of previous row. Make body and sleeves, then unfasten the foundation ch and pick up sts to work single rib toward opposite end. Join shoulder seam inside out with sl st, using crochet hook. Work neckband beforehand, then the center band. Make buttonholes on right front, working 2 sts together with knit st front and 1 casting loop. Sew side and sleeve seam overcasting at each row. Set sleeves in body neatly with sl st using crochet hook.

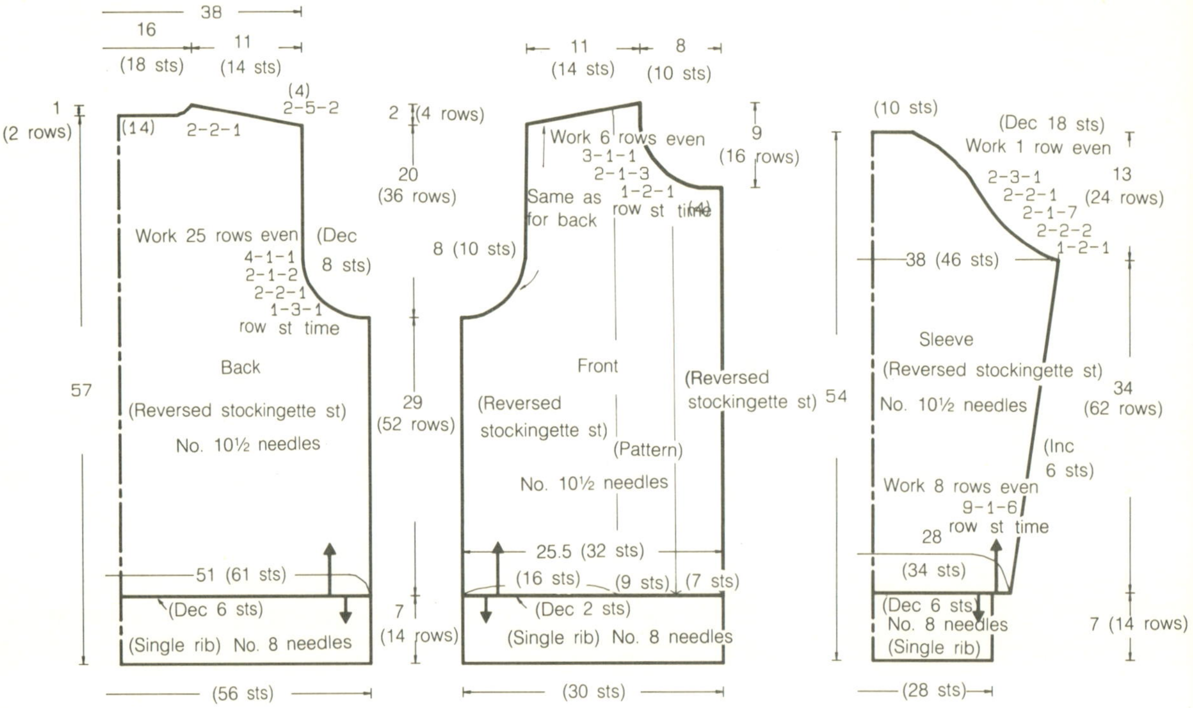

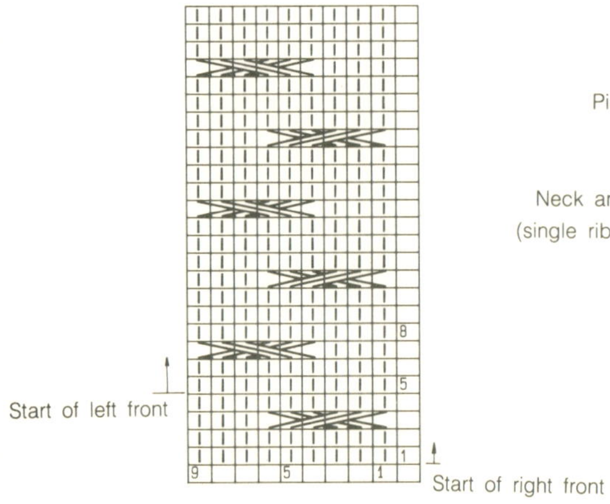

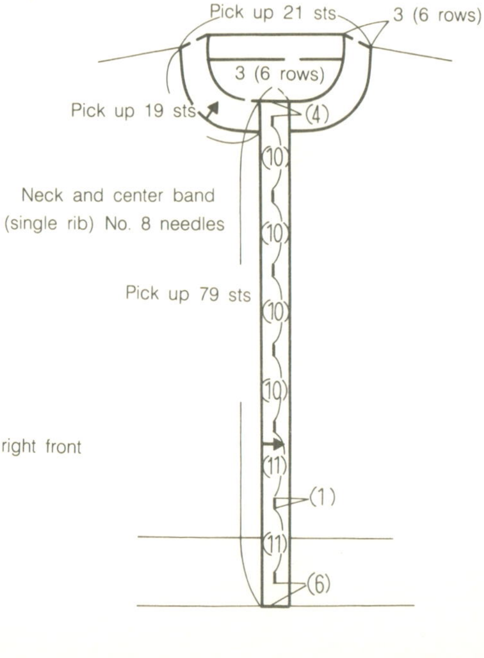

★ **Shown on page 58.**

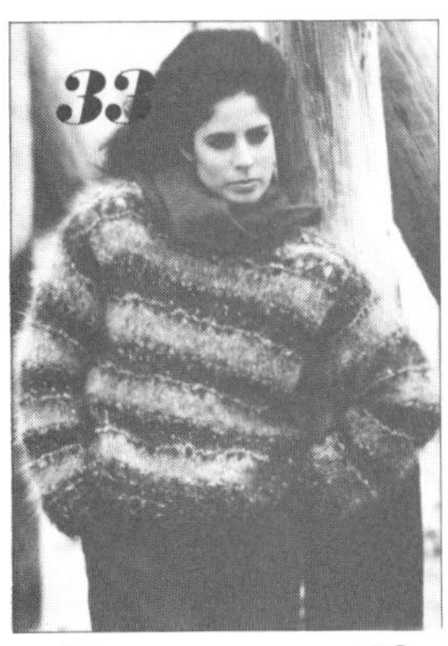

MATERIALS: "Bulky Yarn" 290g yarn variegated red, blue, white, purple, green, etc., and 230g yarn variegated red, beige, pink, white, etc.
NEEDLES: Knitting needles No. 10½.
SIZES: Bust ... 100cm. Width across back measurement ... 40cm. Length ... 55cm. Center of neck to wrist measurement ... 70cm.
GAUGE: 10 sts and 15 rows in 10cm square over pattern B. 10 sts and 16 rows in 10cm square over patterns A and C.
DIRECTIONS: Make ch sts with another yarn using crochet hook, and transfer sts from wrong side of ch to start body and sleeve; then after shaping body and sleeve, unfasten the foundation ch, and finish with sl st using crochet hook on wrong side. Work pattern A to C, noting the change of color. Bind off 5 sts of underarm at the beginning of row on wrong side at first, then the next row on right side. See diagram on page 74 on the method of leaving sts on shoulder slope. Increase sts to shape sleeve, lifting the loop lying 1 st inside both ends of previous row. Place remaining 47 sts of sleeve on holder. Join shoulder seam with sl st and work neckband; then finish with sl st on wrong side. Set sleeve in body grafting sts and rows. (See page 73.) Be sure to pick up 1 st inside from edge of body. Sew side and sleeve seam with overcasting st and complete.

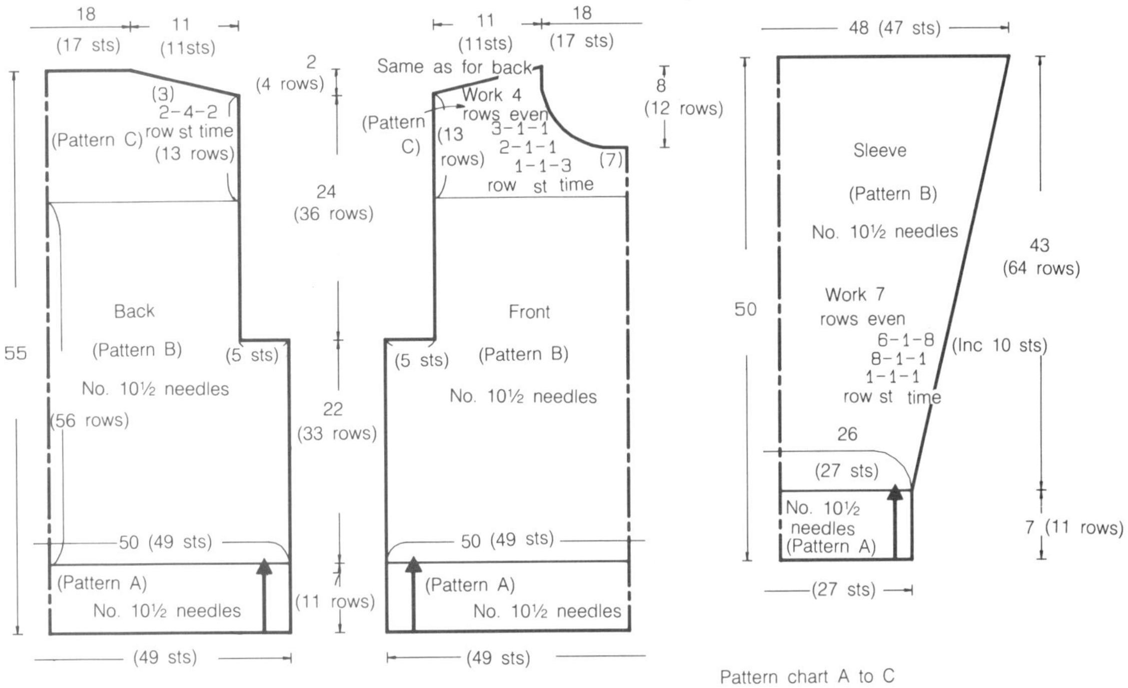

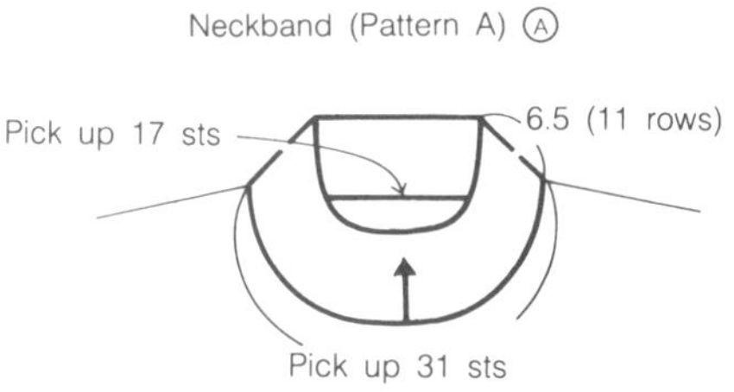

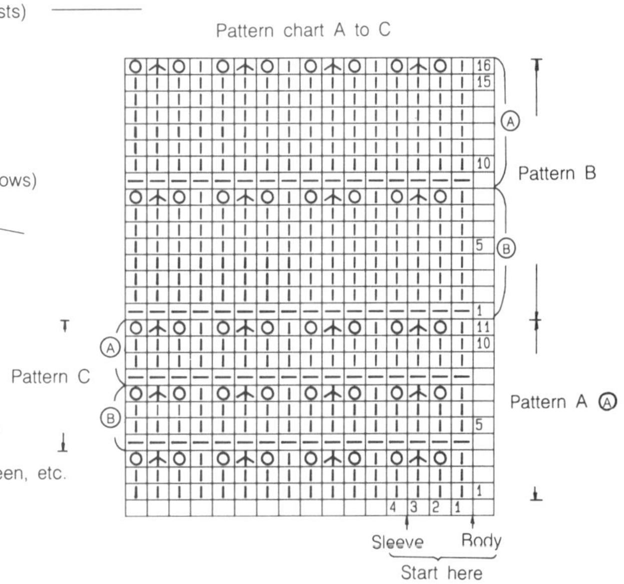

Ⓑ ... Yarn variegated red, beige, pink, white, etc.

Ⓐ ... Yarn variegated red, blue, white, purple, green, etc.

 Continued from page 36.

Ⓐ Increase 1 st on the first row of 2

Ⓑ Cross and knit 2 sts together

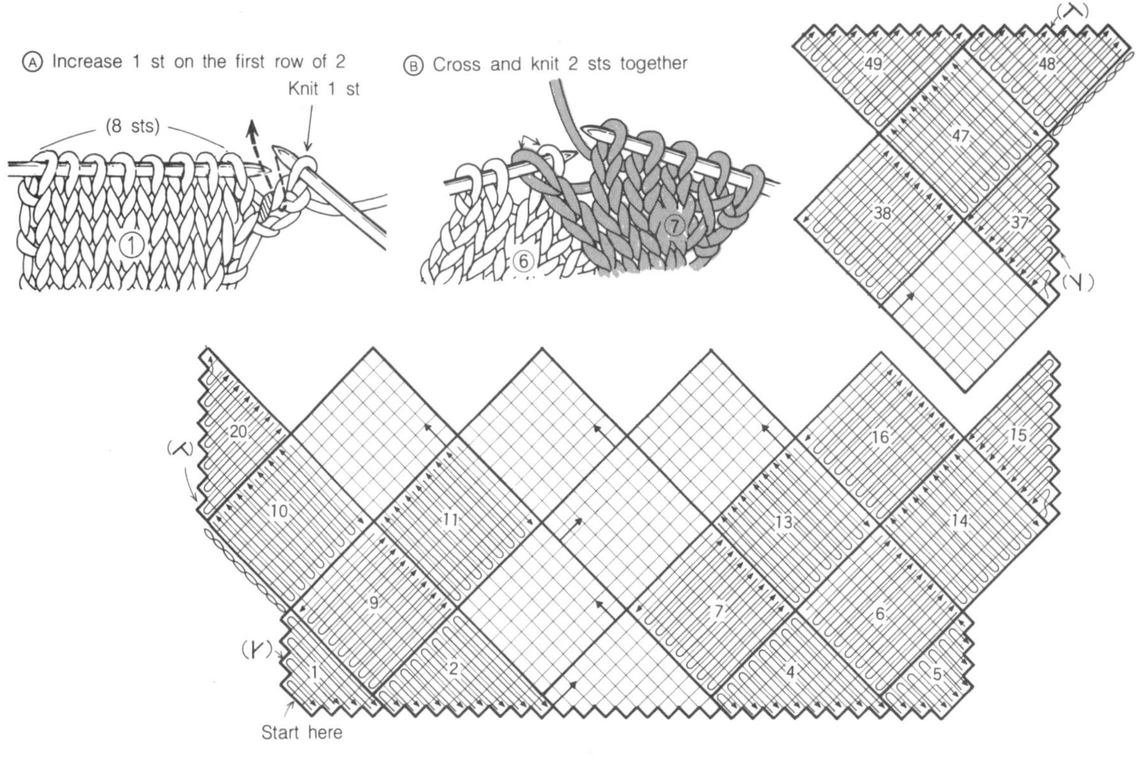

Casting on sts with needles

Making the foundation ch

Decreasing over 2 sts

Increasing st

Grafting sts and rows

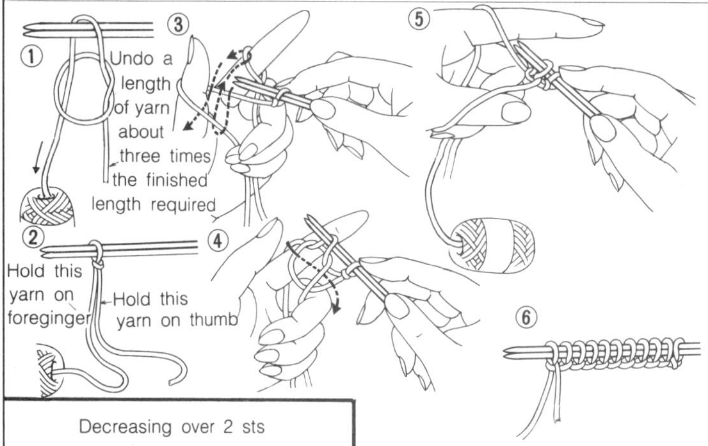

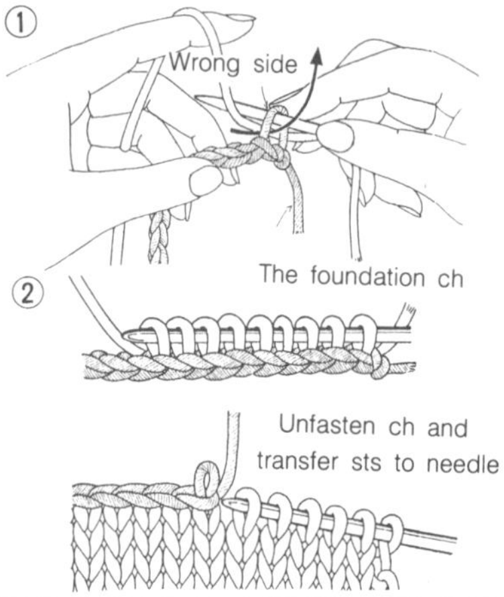

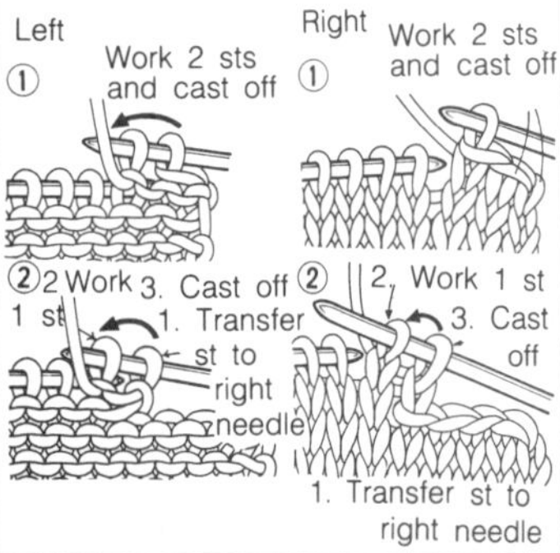

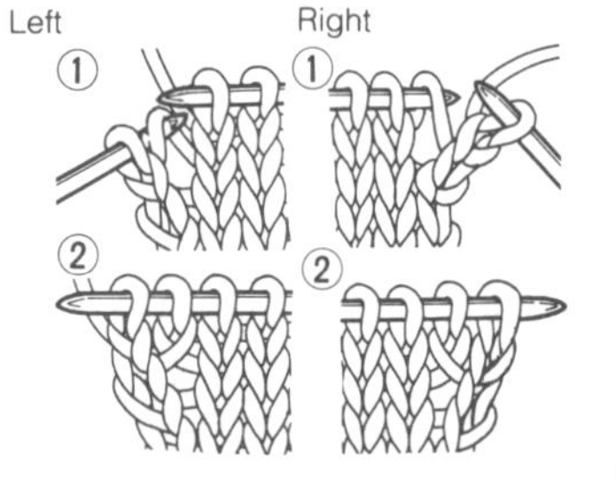

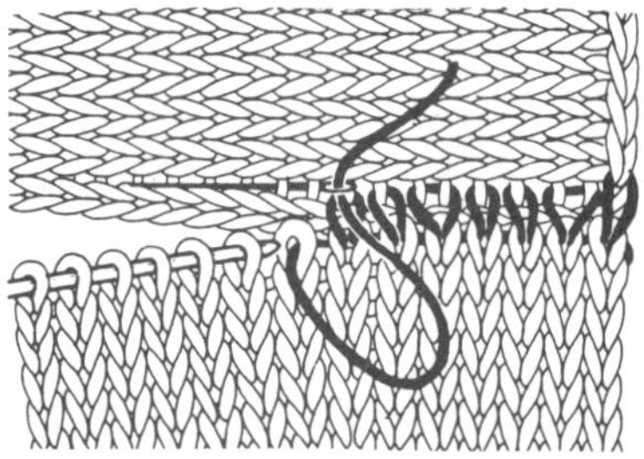

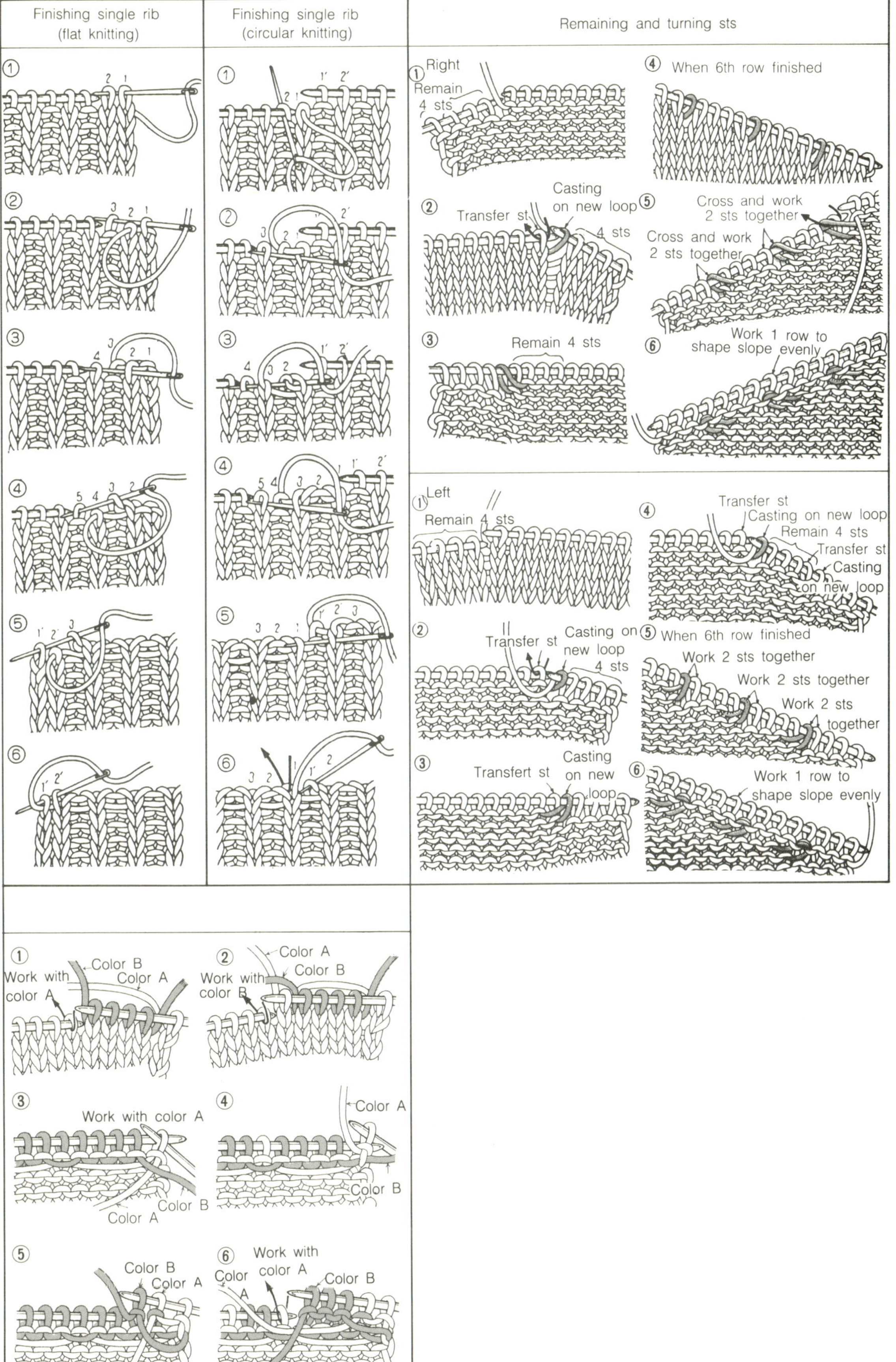

Finishing single rib (flat knitting)
Finishing single rib (circular knitting)
Remaining and turning sts
Right
Remain 4 sts
Transfer st
Casting on new loop
4 sts
Remain 4 sts
When 6th row finished
Cross and work 2 sts together
Cross and work 2 sts together
Work 1 row to shape slope evenly
Left
Remain 4 sts
Transfer st
Casting on new loop
4 sts
Transfer st
Casting on new loop
Remain 4 sts
Transfer st
Casting on new loop
When 6th row finished
Work 2 sts together
Work 2 sts together
Work 2 sts together
Transfert st
Casting on new loop
Work 1 row to shape slope evenly
Work with color A
Color B
Color A
Work with color B
Color A
Color B
Work with color A
Color A
Color B
Color A
Color B
Color B
Color A
Work with color A
Color B

Basic Techniques and Symbols

These are generally accepted symbols. Learn the meaning of the symbols and their procedures. You will be able to make patterns by combining several of these symbols.

Knit stitch

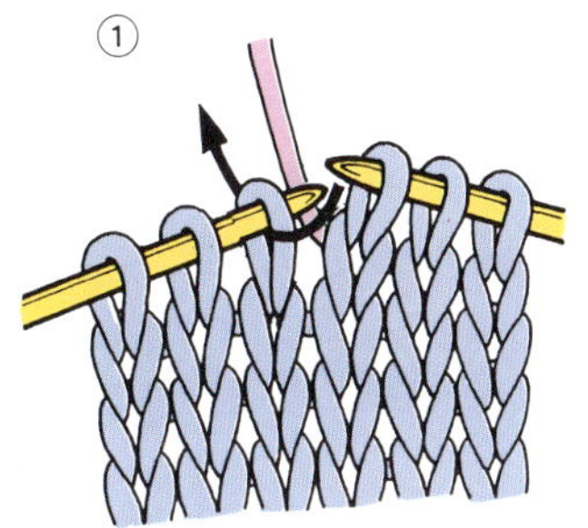 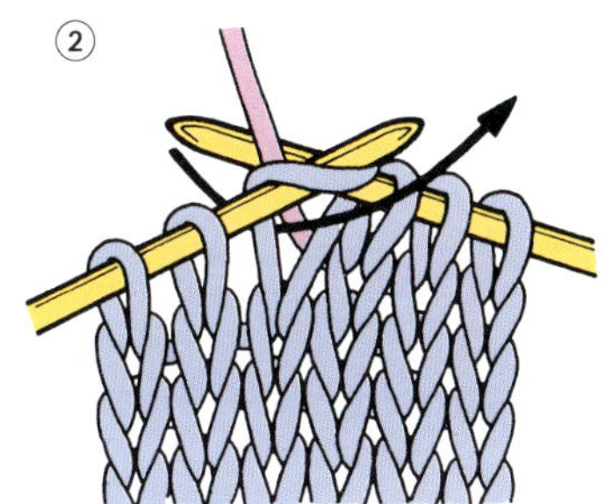 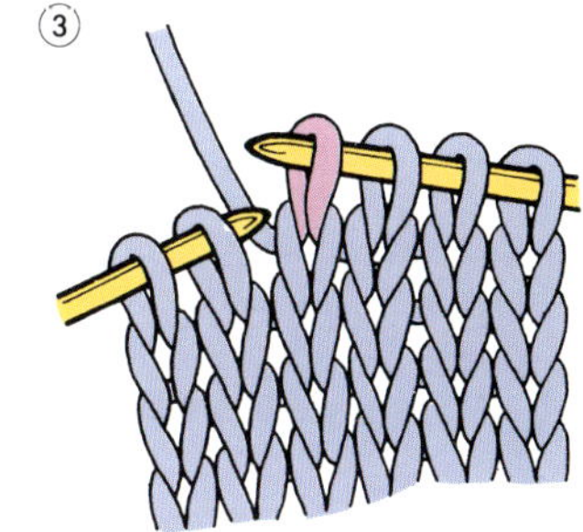

Purl stitch

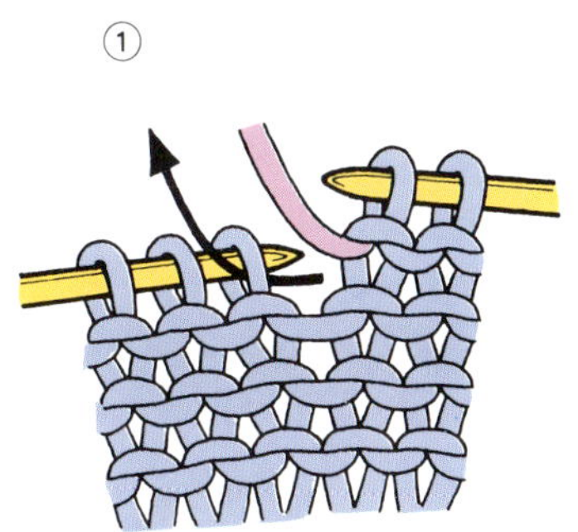 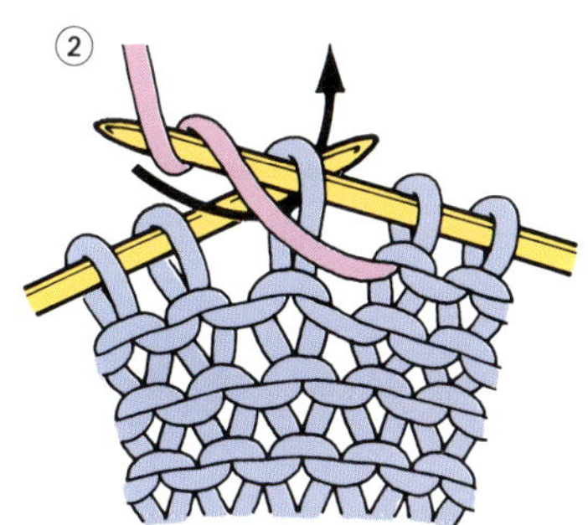 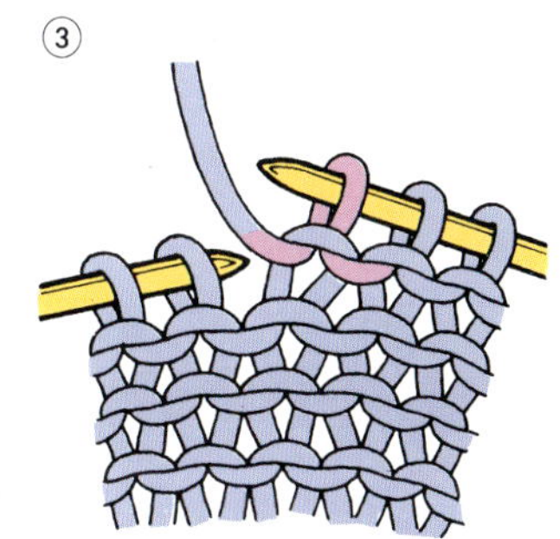

Cast on new loop between 2 stitches.

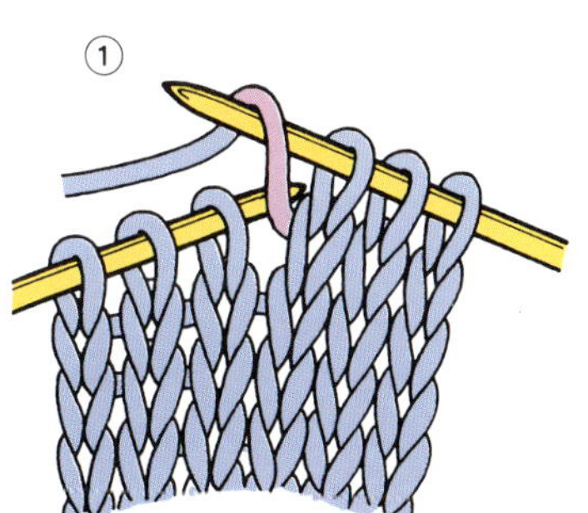 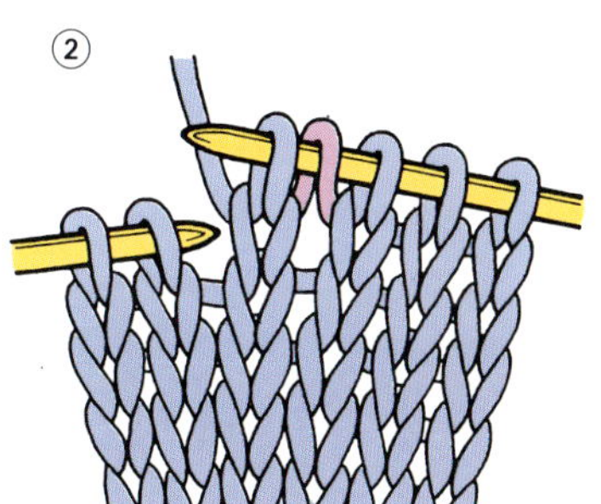 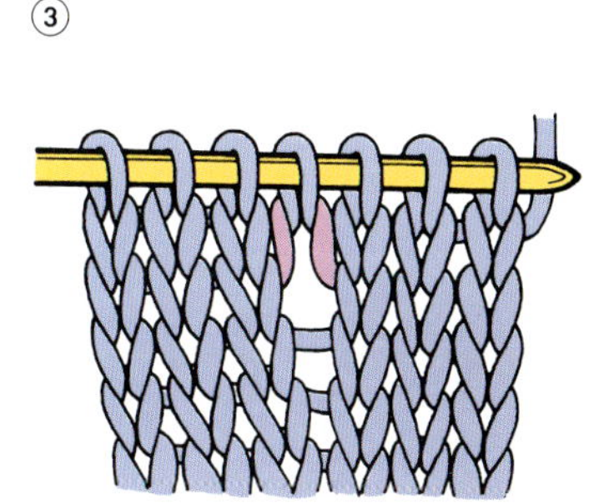

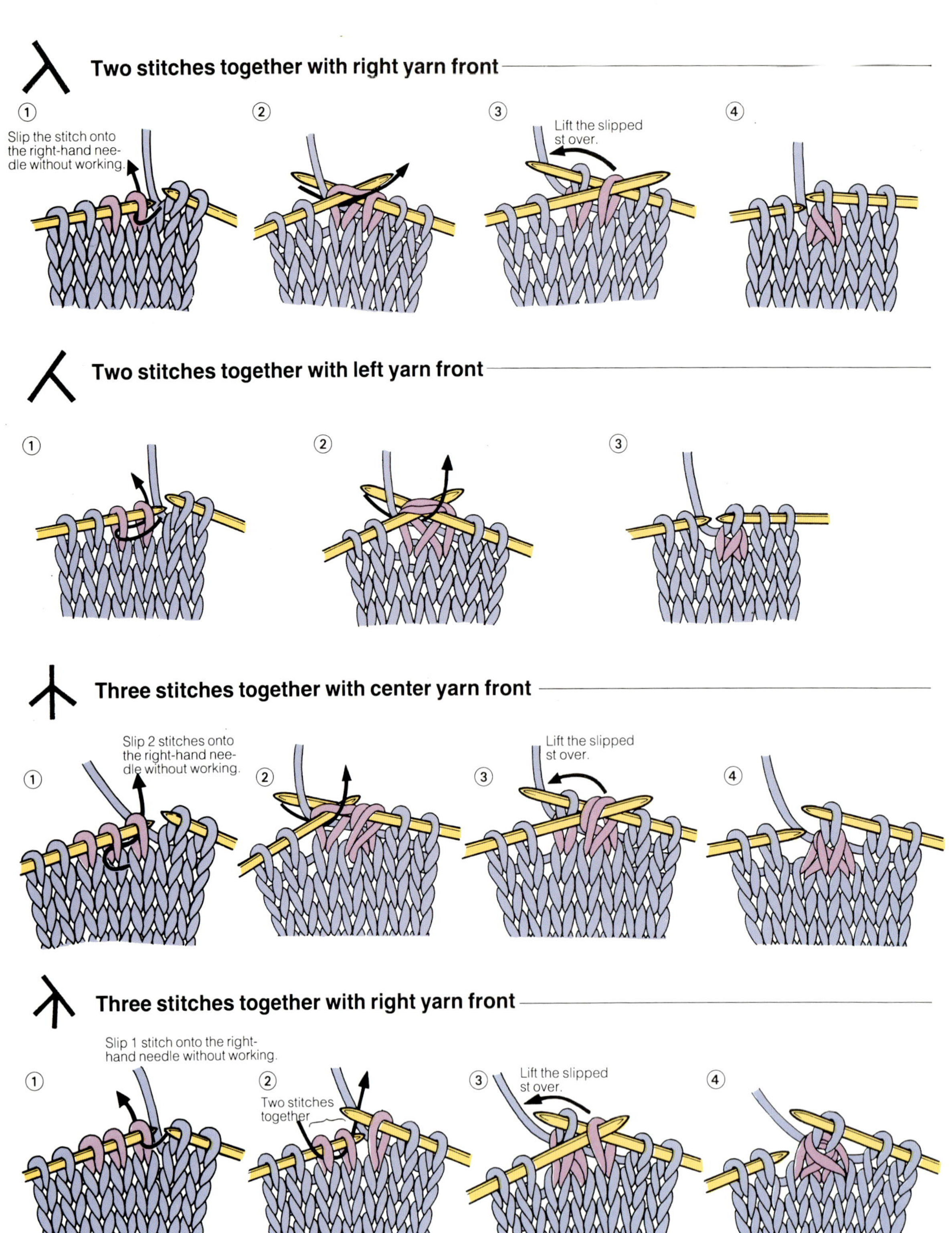

Two stitches together with right yarn front
1
Slip the stitch onto the right-hand needle without working.
2
3
Lift the slipped st over.
4
Two stitches together with left yarn front
1
2
3
Three stitches together with center yarn front
1
Slip 2 stitches onto the right-hand needle without working.
2
3
Lift the slipped st over.
4
Three stitches together with right yarn front
1
Slip 1 stitch onto the right-hand needle without working.
2
Two stitches together
3
Lift the slipped st over.
4

Three stitches together with left yarn front

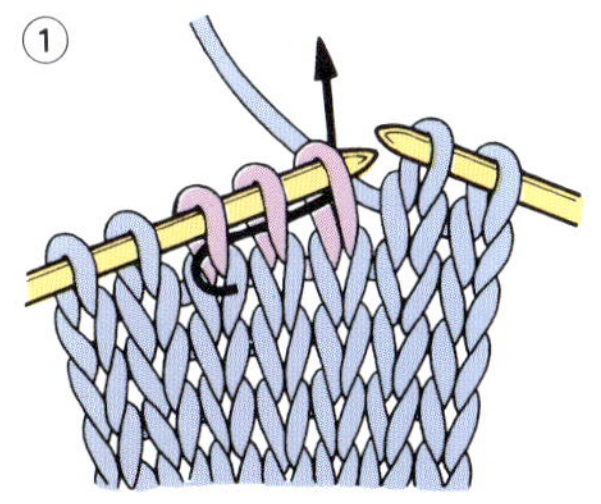

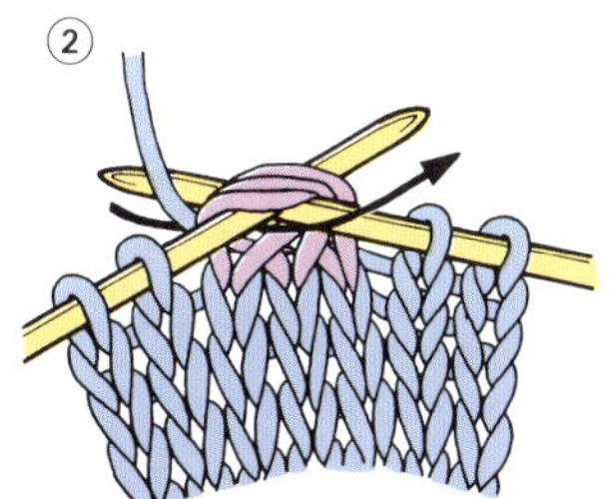

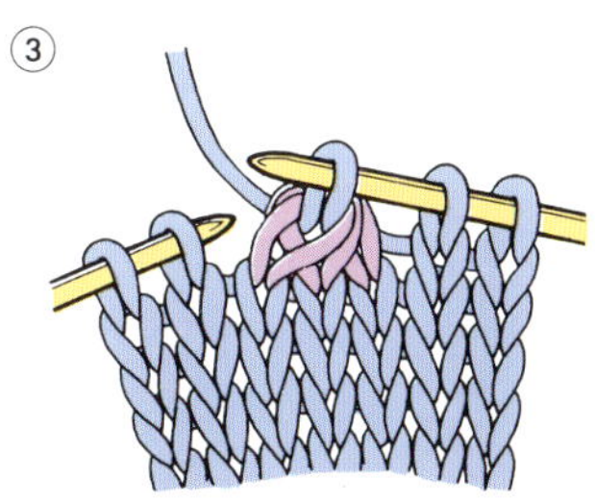

Increase stitches working into 1 stitch.

(Increase the number (3 sts) of sts working into 1 st.)

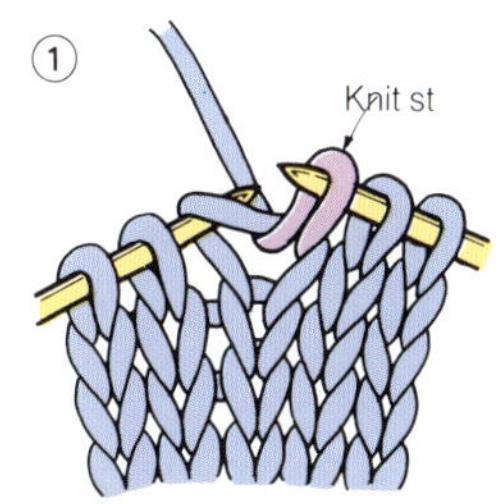

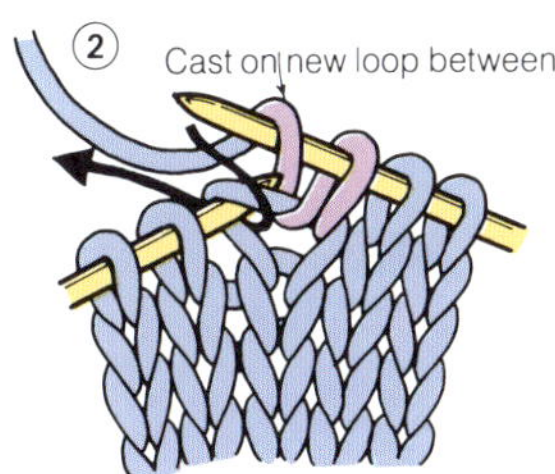

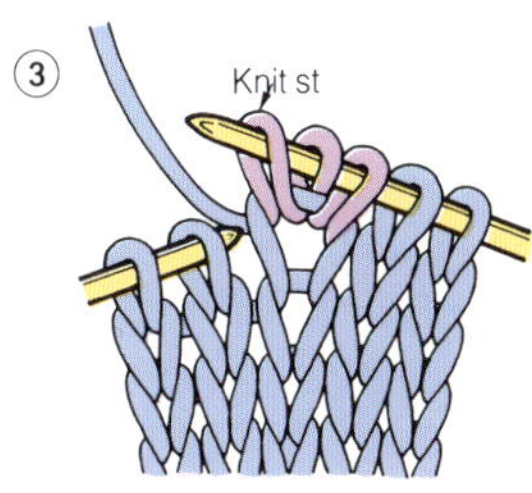

Intersect with right stitch front.

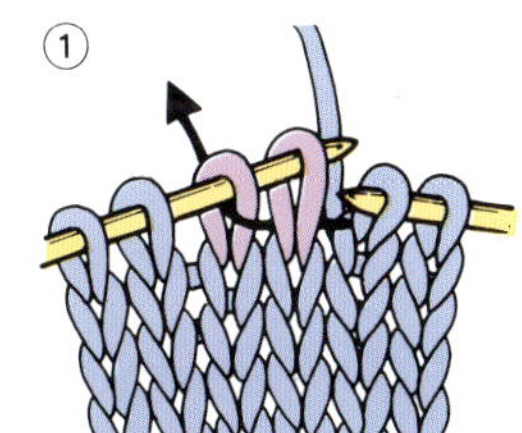

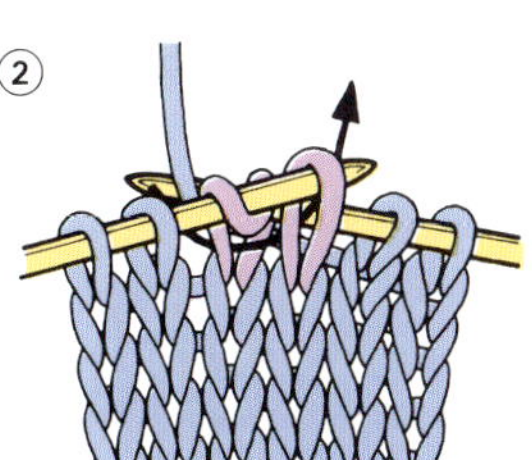

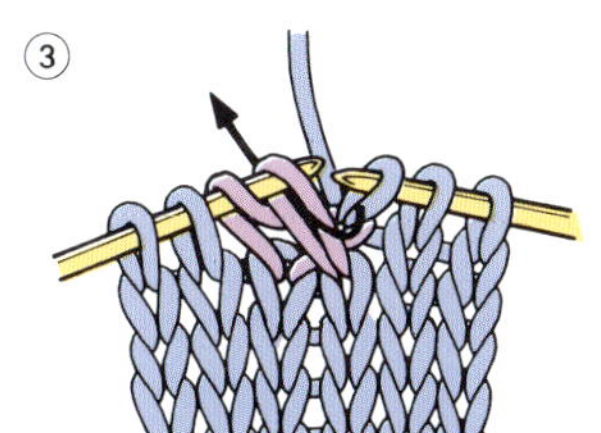

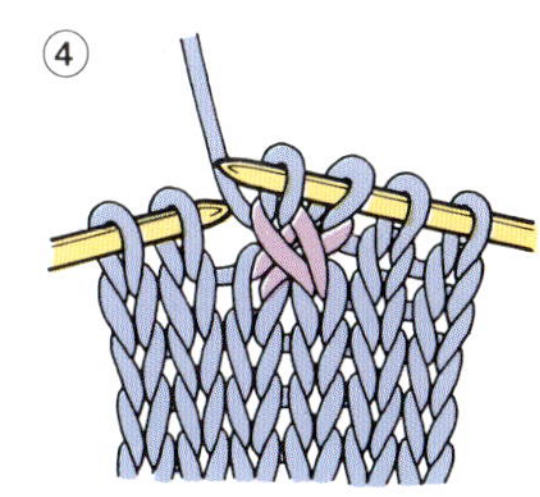

Intersect with left stitch front.

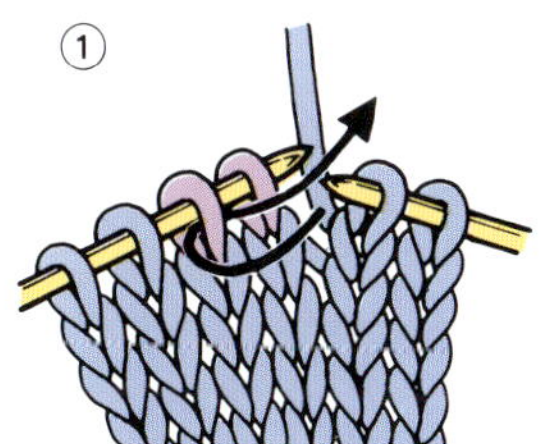

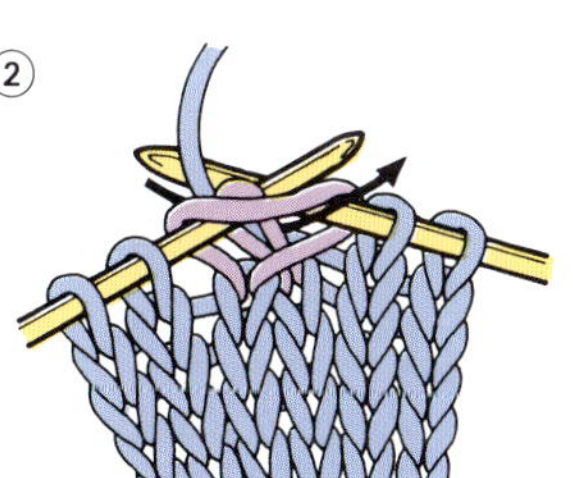

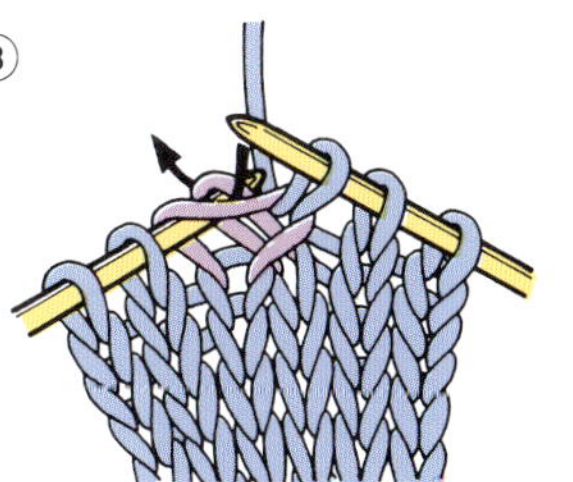

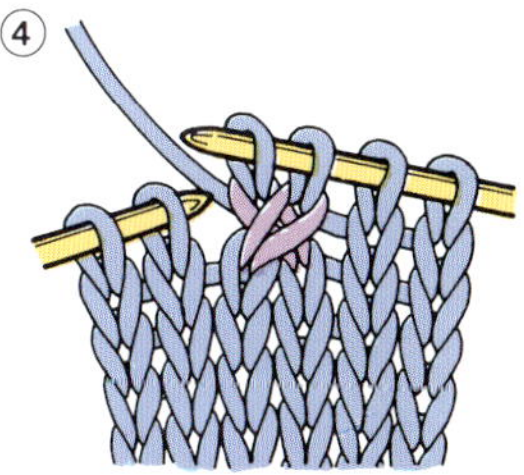

V Pass slipped stitch over.

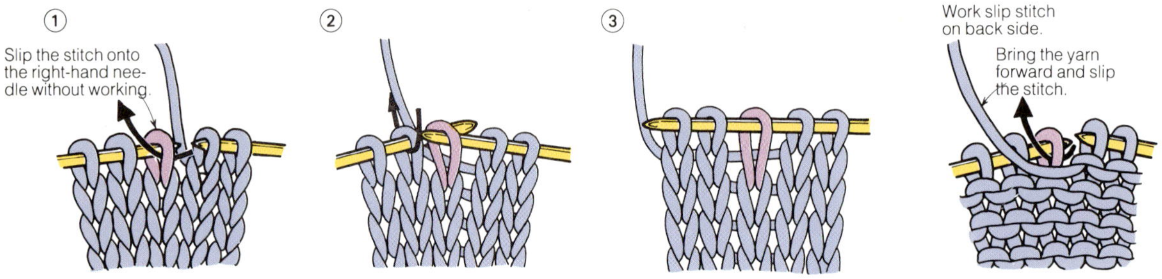

① Slip the stitch onto the right-hand needle without working.

②

③

Work slip stitch on back side.
Bring the yarn forward and slip the stitch.

∀ Pass slipped stitch over, bringing the yarn forward.

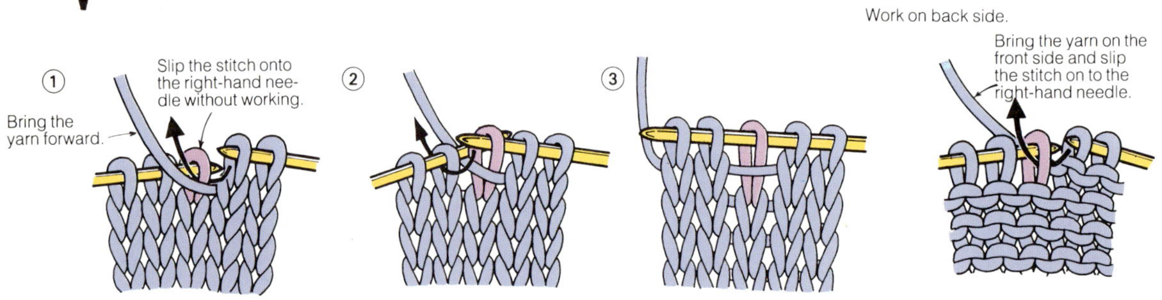

① Bring the yarn forward. Slip the stitch onto the right-hand needle without working.

②

③

Work on back side.
Bring the yarn on the front side and slip the stitch on to the right-hand needle.

Ọ Twisted stitch

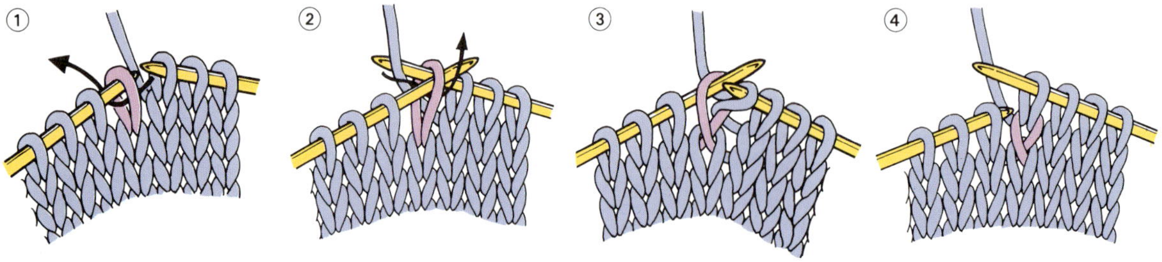

①

②

③

④

∩ Raised stitch

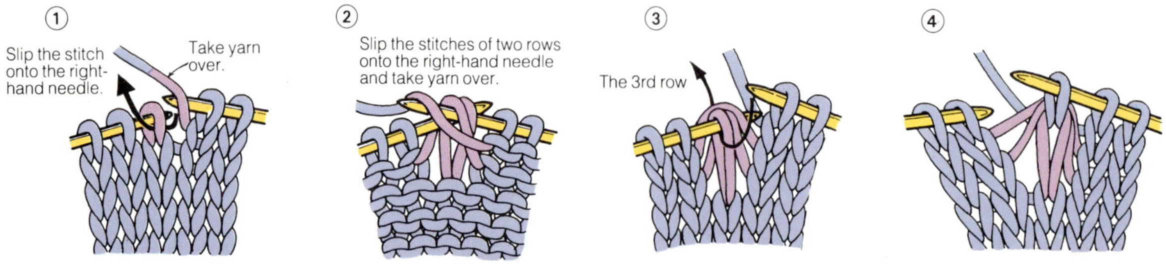

① Slip the stitch onto the right-hand needle. Take yarn over.

② Slip the stitches of two rows onto the right-hand needle and take yarn over.

③ The 3rd row

④